AN
UNCOMMON
THEORY

OF
SCHOOL CHANGE

AN
UNCOMMON
THEORY

OF
SCHOOL CHANGE

LEADERSHIP FOR REINVENTING SCHOOLS

KEVIN FAHEY, ANGELA BREIDENSTEIN,
JACY IPPOLITO, AND FRANCES HENSLEY

FOREWORD BY JOSEPH P. MCDONALD

TEACHERS COLLEGE PRESS

TEACHERS COLLEGE | COLUMBIA UNIVERSITY

NEW YORK AND LONDON

Published by Teachers College Press, 1234 Amsterdam Avenue, New York, NY 10027

Cover design by Jeremy Fink.

The authors express gratitude for permission to use the following:

Tables 3.1 and 3.2 are from *Leading for Powerful Learning: A Guide for Instructional Leaders* by A. Breidenstein, K. Fahey, C. Glickman, and F. Hensley, 2012, New York, NY, Teachers College Press. Used with permission.

Table 4.1 is adapted with permission from Ippolito, J. (2013). Professional learning as the key to linking content and literacy instruction. In J. Ippolito, J. F. Lawrence, and C. Zaller, (Eds.), *Adolescent literacy in the era of the common core: From research into practice* (pp. 215–234). Cambridge, MA: Harvard Education Press.

Figure 6.1 is adapted from *American School Reform: What Works, What Fails, and Why* by J. P. McDonald, 2014, Chicago, IL: University of Chicago Press.

Library of Congress Cataloging-in-Publication Data

Names: Fahey, Kevin, author. I Breidenstein, Angela, author. I Ippolito, Jacy, author. I Hensley, Frances, author. I McDonald, Joseph P., author of foreword.
Title: An uncommon theory of school change : leadership for reinventing schools / Kevin Fahey, Angela Breidenstein, Jacy Ippolito, and Frances Hensley ; foreword by Joseph P. McDonald.
Description: New York, NY : Teachers College Press, [2019] I Includes bibliographical references and index. I
Identifiers: LCCN 2018060735 (print) I LCCN 2019004566 (ebook) I ISBN 9780807777657 (ebook) I ISBN 9780807761243 (pbk.) I ISBN 9780807777657 (ebk.)
Subjects: LCSH: Educational change. I Educational leadership.
Classification: LCC LB2806 (ebook) I LCC LB2806 .F35 2019 (print) I DDC 371.2/07—dc23
LC record available at https://lccn.loc.gov/2018060735

ISBN 978-0-8077-6124-3 (paper)
ISBN 978-0-8077-6173-1 (hardcover)
ISBN 978-0-8077-7765-7 (ebook)

Printed on acid-free paper

Manufactured in the United States of America

26 25 24 23 22 21 20 19   8 7 6 5 4 3 2 1

Contents

Foreword

Here is an invitation to dive into the deepest and murkiest educational waters—where certainties about schooling and its improvement dissolve, where often unnoticed but very live cultures swarm and complicate change efforts, turning many of them into muck. This invitation may not sound inviting. But the destination it proposes is the place where the real relations that comprise schooling, teaching, and learning are most visible and touchable. These relations are the ones that connect teachers to their subjects and to each other or not, the ones that encourage students to persevere or give up, the ones that undergird parents' trust or distrust. This is where one can best discern whether a school's stated ambition for its impact is authentic or fake, and in either case why. This is the place where a school and its community can identify its real needs and figure out how best to meet them.

The book presents in IMAX intensity how to make this jump. It will show you vividly what to expect on the way down, and explain clearly how to exploit the strategic advantage of going so deep. Yes, the dives the authors advocate can be risky, and may provoke anxiety in your settings that will be challenging to manage. But, as the authors explain, such anxiety can be managed, and they show how—through ample preparation, shallow diving before deep diving, and the fostering of a sense of *we-ness* (no lone diving!). The payoff for this effort is significant, particularly now when equity-focused ambition for *all* students' understanding, making, doing, and dreaming is accelerating, and when confidence in the simple installation of school improvement from a distance (forced at the point of a data spreadsheet) is diminishing. Happily, there are openings in the zeitgeist now for thoughtful educational activists—backed by we-ness and a willingness to take and manage risks—to gather the resources school reinvention needs: sufficient professional capacity, political and civic support, and money enough to do more than the same old things.

Meanwhile, this book will serve as a trusty coaching guide. The writing is clear and powerful. The testimony of the courageous and inventive school practitioners the authors studied is rich and exceedingly useful. And, by the way, you will learn their real names: You can contact them if you want to. The signage the authors supply for the diving—the graphics and tables, the sheer organization of the chapters—is among the best I've ever seen in a book about school reform. But wait. Before you read much further, I recommend one preparatory task. Given the centrality of we-ness to school reinvention and the challenge of achieving and sustaining it, and given the intensity of this book, I suggest you find at least one reading partner to join you in this read. It may be a colleague (or two) from your work setting, or it may be a friend who works elsewhere but will respond to your text messages as you read, and will join you eagerly in the sense making of reading, in figuring out how to act in your respective contexts. Think of yourselves not just as preparing to dive, but also as helping to build a movement of divers.

Joseph P. McDonald

Preface

This is a book for activists. It is for educators who not only think schools need to be improved, but are also fiercely committed to their reinvention and hopeful that it can be achieved. We have written this book to support them and keep their hope alive.

This is a book that looks at the most difficult work that school leaders do: questioning, rethinking, and reenacting the most fundamental assumptions upon which our schools are built. We call this work the *deep dive*. It is through the deep dive that educators develop collective capacity to investigate hidden assumptions, manage the pressure that the exploration creates, and discern an emerging better future, even when the future cannot be clearly seen. None of this is easy or common.

This book has a threefold focus. First, it addresses the issue of why educators can no longer expect to "improve" their way to the schools their students truly need. We outline the difference between improvement and reinvention from organizational and leadership points of view to help leaders have a clearer understanding of what each can—and cannot—achieve.

Second, it shares the stories of a diverse group of courageous school leaders who have embraced activism and accepted the challenge, risk, and joy of developing a complex leadership practice. We believe these stories of their strength and vulnerability will resonate with readers as it did with us.

Third, the book describes a broad repertoire of tools, strategies, and techniques these activist leaders used effectively in their important work. While providing practical methods, it also offers insight into the complexities of school reinvention.

We believe there is a place for hope, and this book is a hopeful book. Our hope resides in these activist educators and in the power of their reinvention efforts. We hope that sharing their stories and a framework for their deep dives into reinvention will inspire hope and action among other educators of every title and role to see themselves as leaders and co-enactors of the more transformational change of reinvention. As Rosi Braidotti (2013) describes it, "hope is a way of dreaming up possible futures; an anticipatory virtue that permeates our lives and activates them"

(p. 12). For Andres Lopez, one of our profiled leaders who teaches high school English and is pioneering a Mexican American Literature course in San Antonio, Texas, this anticipatory virtue and possible future sound like this:

> I considered becoming a lawyer to fight for equitable resources for urban schools or becoming a policymaker to champion legislation that would improve the educational system. Ultimately, I chose teaching. Not only was it a concrete way to serve my community through my talents and motivations of understanding and motivating urban youth, but it was also fertile ground in which to help students grow and prepare them for the challenges I knew awaited them. Youth I've encountered have boundless dreams, and I challenge myself every day to make those possible. When teachers find a way to make this happen, they will see their students' brilliance, creativity, love, and passion. Through their students, they will see, as I do every day, how the human story goes on and replenishes the spirit and resolve of those who know where to look.

We seek to engage and activate hope, so that this book might serve to kindle and replenish the spirit, resolve, and practice of leaders and schools seeking an UnCommon approach to leadership and school reinvention in order to create a better, more just, more equitable future for each and all of our students.

Acknowledgments

The heart of this book is the stories of nine activist leaders who generously shared their own deep dives. We thank Deborah Holman, Jed Lippard, Andres Lopez, Michael Maloney, Cathy O'Connell, Liz Ozuna, Andy Plemmons, Matt Underwood, and Deirdre Williams. We are indebted to Joe McDonald for not only writing the Foreword to this book, but also for the clear thinking and rigorous scholarship that characterizes the entire body of his work, which informs and inspires our writing team. We are also indebted to the external reviewers and editorial board at Teachers College Press whose feedback challenged and affirmed our thinking and helped shape this book. We deeply appreciate Ileana Rivera Liberatore and Jim Okey for their insightful questions and comments as they read the manuscript. Finally, we thank Teachers College Press, especially Carole Saltz, for their faith in and commitment to this project and their encouragement to take on a deeper follow-up to our earlier book, *Leading for Powerful Learning* (Breidenstein, Fahey, Glickman, & Hensley, 2012).

CHAPTER 1

Navigating the Waters of School Change

> . . . all successful schools have followed the same proven formula: higher standards, more accountability, and extra help so children who need it can get it to reach those standards.
>
> —President Bill Clinton, State of the Union Address, January 27, 2000

> It still feels like every time you're walking out on air when you say "We're not going to do test prep—we're going to do great teaching." We're going to build kids' confidence in their skills and learning, and that's going to get them through whatever assessment they face—not just the state test, but an interview, a portfolio, the SAT.
>
> —Liz Ozuna

Cathy O'Connell, Principal of North Reading Middle School in North Reading, Massachusetts, followed what she called a "recipe" when she tried to implement the Multi-Tiered System of Supports (MTSS) framework for tiered instruction at her school (Positive Behavioral Interventions and Support, 2018). In her mind, test data indicated that a structure such as MTSS was needed, and MTSS aligned closely with new district and state goals. Cathy explained, "We said we were going to implement MTSS, and we paid somebody to come in and explain it and work with faculty, a really nice guy, certainly knew his stuff." Following her common recipe, Cathy saw a clear need and hired a consultant. Yet, during what seemed to be a routine program implementation, Assistant Principal Michael Maloney candidly admitted, "Teachers didn't make the connections at all. Really, it was a nightmare." Cathy added, "They instantly felt like it was a waste of their time."

Cathy and Michael's recipe—used widely in our nation's schools— began a multiyear conversation for our writing team around two essential questions:

- Why does the widely used strategy of identifying problems and finding programs, initiatives, and curricula to address the problem seem to yield such meager results?
- How does deep reform that not only improves schools, but actually reinvents them, happen?

As we began thinking about these questions and this book, we scanned the dense landscape of educational leadership and school change literature. We found many books about school *improvement* (e.g., Blase, Blase, & Philips, 2010; Kramer & Schuhl, 2017) and many more about school *reform* (e.g., Elmore, 2004; McDonald, 2014; Tienken & Orlich, 2013). We even found a handful of books about school *transformation* (e.g., Aguilar, 2013; Benitez, Davidson, & Flaxman, 2009). The research and practice landscape is vast and complicated, full of good ideas and useful advice.

When we delved deeper, other simple but inescapable questions surfaced: "Are school *improvement*, *reform*, and *transformation* the same? Versions of each other? Or even quite different and separate concepts?" As we talked to a diverse group of school leaders, we realized that these leaders often worked simultaneously on issues of improvement, reform, and even school transformation. They also used these terms interchangeably and in a variety of ways. We asked ourselves, "What is our new book *really* going to be about?"

Very quickly we decided this would not be a book about school improvement or reform. It would definitely not be a book about new and improved programs. This would be a book about, and for, school leaders who take up the challenge of rethinking and reinventing their schools' most fundamental assumptions and deepest practices. These assumptions might include the very purpose of schools, the nature of equitable educational practice, what it means to be a teacher and a student, or practices such as how students are organized for instruction or how curriculum is developed. This became a book about school *reinvention*.

The school leaders whose voices inform this book understand that schools certainly need to be improved, reformed, and maybe even transformed. Yet, at a deeper level, they know that schools desperately need to be reinvented. As mentioned in the Preface, this is a book for school leaders who are interested in taking a deep dive into school reinvention— a dive that produces anxiety, challenges everyone to be better, and disturbs closely held cultural assumptions.

THE 21st-CENTURY CONTEXT FOR SCHOOLS

Broadly speaking, at the outset of the 21st century, two profound societal shifts are influencing the work of educators. First, the world has become a more complicated and interconnected place, and our students need knowledge, skills, and dispositions that previously had rarely been required (Darling-Hammond, 2010). Instead of reporting on what scientists have learned, students are now expected to do the work of scientists; rather than memorizing what historians have discovered, they are now asked to do the

> A fear was that we could not change the culture of our school and our small town to expect kids would be successful.
>
> —Liz Ozuna

work of historians. Students are routinely asked to consider a variety of perspectives on complex issues, craft persuasive arguments, and then design and build models, projects, and simulations to test their hypotheses. In general, the model of content-centered schools no longer serves our children well, especially in an age when content is just something to be downloaded from a cell phone.

Second, students themselves have changed, have become more complicated, and present a range of identities, many of which were not acknowledged a few decades ago. In the 1980s it may have made sense to talk about "homogeneous grouping" and "honors, college prep, and standard" levels of classes. Now, all classes include students with a range of learning strengths and challenges; in some classes there are students who struggle to learn English and students who speak many languages; in other classes are students who are struggling with gender identity. As in the past, classes today include students who are socially adept and students who are socially challenged; gifted readers and students with no interest in reading; students with strong religious convictions and students with none; students who are eager for the school day to begin and students who are eager for it to end; students from the most privileged environments and students who enjoy very little, if any, privilege. In today's schools, students present a wide range of identities, interests, learning profiles, and life circumstances, and they are asked to perform at increasingly higher levels.

Furthermore, there is a predictive value attached to the identities of many of our students. Often race, class, gender, sexual orientation, language, and learning differences have clear correlations with student success and college, career, and life outcomes (Bachman, Staff, O'Malley, & Freedman-Doan, 2013; Farkas, 2017; Kurtz-Costes, Swinton, & Skinner, 2014). The challenge facing educators is daunting. This book is for educators who accept this formidable challenge; who understand and are horrified by the predictive value of such things as race, class, and gender; and who want to develop their capacity and the capacity of their schools to let go of the patterns of the past and allow a new, more equitable future to emerge.

WHAT IS THE COMMON THEORY FOR IMPROVING SCHOOLS?

In many ways, the theory of action for improving and reforming our nation's schools is plainly visible and commonly held. It is articulated by policymakers including presidents, shaped by state educational bureaucracies, approved by local school boards, implemented by principals and teachers, and researched and measured by academics, all in the service of students. Presidents Obama, Bush, and Clinton have agreed that what we refer to as the *Common Theory*

> We are transforming our schools by raising standards and focusing on results.
> —*President George W. Bush, Republican Convention Acceptance Speech, September 2, 2004*

of action for improving schools is comprised of large quantities of higher standards, increased accountability, and best practices. This Common Theory normally contains rigor, professional development, data-driven decisionmaking, and high-stakes testing (McDonald, Isacoff, & Karin, 2018). The Common Theory is well known.

At the school level, the Common Theory of school reform looks something like this: First, a need is identified. Often, needs are connected to issues with test scores or other data such as graduation rates or attendance. Second, a strategy to address the need is chosen. Often this strategy takes the form of something new—a new plan, system, or intervention—for example, a new literacy initiative or bullying-prevention plan. Speaking generally, schools and districts tend to buy a program, initiative, or curriculum that addresses the identified need.

In the third step of the Common Theory, the district or school provides, often with the help of an outside consultant, professional development for the educators, who are supposed to implement the program that addresses the identified need. So, for example, when a district decides to implement Universal Design for Learning (UDL) (Rose & Meyer, 2006), at least some teachers predictably go to workshops and learn about UDL and how it should look in their classrooms. Districts implementing guided reading programs send teachers to learn about strategies that work, or in other cases bring an expert into the school to coach them about the practice. While most districts claim that professional learning is an important goal, research shows that step 3 of the Common Theory is carried out in a variety of ways and with a range of results (Chung Wei, Darling-Hammond, & Adamson, 2010; Guskey & Yoon, 2009; McDonald et al., 2018).

> But we know that our schools don't just need more resources. They need more reform.
> —*President Barack Obama, Address to Joint Session of Congress, February 24, 2009*

Step 4 of the Common Theory is implementation. Teachers are expected to return to their classrooms and implement the new practice, curriculum, program, or initiative. The Common Theory typically has very little to say about how this essential step is carried out.

The last two steps of the Common Theory, accountability and measurement, are often conflated. After a need is identified, strategy selected, and professional development provided, then teachers, principals, and schools are held accountable for carrying out the strategy. Fidelity of implementation is important in the Common Theory. Principals, department heads, and other evaluative personnel are asked, for example, to ensure that inquiry-based science instruction is being done *correctly*, Response to Intervention (RtI) is being *implemented with fidelity*, or the new schedule is running *efficiently*. Accountability is a key ingredient of the Common Theory, and consequences (either explicit or implied) are often attached to implementation.

> The big idea of school accountability ... was built around three principles: creating rigorous academic standards, measuring student progress against those standards, and attaching some consequence to the results.
>
> —*President George W. Bush, Republican Convention Acceptance Speech, September 2, 2004*

Measurement is also important. After teachers are held accountable, the same principal—although occasionally an outside evaluator— is asked to collect data to determine if the strategy and its implementation did in fact address the identified need. Although measurement is not always carried out effectively (if at all), the Common Theory demands that schools measure their results (McDonald et al., 2018). No district leader would publicly reject the Common Theory and announce that they intend to implement a new initiative, curriculum, program, or structure with no intention of measuring the results. In reality, however, many do just that.

In summary, the Common Theory of school reform widely used by superintendents, principals, school board members, politicians, and even U.S. presidents states that in order to improve, schools need to do the following things:

1. Identify—with the help of data and standards—a need
2. Choose a program, initiative, curriculum, or structure that will address the need
3. Provide some professional learning about the new initiative, program, curriculum, or structure
4. Implement the initiative
5. Hold teachers accountable for faithful implementation
6. Measure the results

Figure 1.1. The Common Theory of School Reform

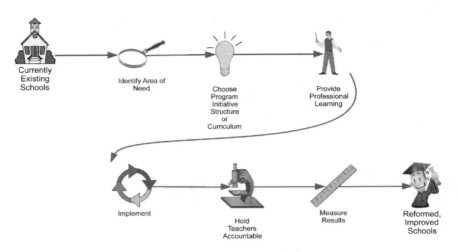

Figure 1.1 summarizes the Common Theory of school reform.

The Common Theory is straightforward and enjoys great popularity with politicians, policymakers, and bureaucrats. There is often considerable pressure on educators to embrace it. The Common Theory can produce useful programs and initiatives that do indeed improve certain aspects of schooling. However, the theory may not have much to do with how schools actually work.

The Common Theory in the Real World of Schools

At North Reading Middle School, the MTSS initiative imploded not because the Common Theory was incorrectly applied, but because Cathy and Michael did not consider the invisible forces that are at work in all organizations, and particularly in schools. Cathy further explained:

> The teachers had no idea why we were doing this. We didn't spend the upfront time unpacking the need. We didn't allow them to discover the need. We didn't allow them to play with the need. We told them there was a need. They didn't buy it, and therefore they didn't buy anything that came after the need.

The Common Theory holds that a need has to be identified, but Cathy and Michael discovered the hard way that the need not only has to be identified, but also unpacked, discovered, played with, and owned by the entire school community. A shared understanding had to be established. Cathy and Michael found that their reform effort was limited by not-so-visible assumptions, a range of capacities, varied frames of reference, longstanding school traditions, competing expectations, hidden rules, and unspoken norms that exist in every school.

The Common Theory at the Bottom of the Harbor

Much of the thinking, drafting, researching, and debating that informs this book took place in a small office that overlooks the harbor in Gloucester, Massachusetts. Gloucester has been a seaport since 1623, and the harbor is filled with a working fishing fleet and surrounded by a colorful waterfront, a frequent subject for generations of American artists. However, many visitors to Gloucester do not understand that beneath the sleek sailboats and picturesque scenes, there exists a crowded—and not nearly as picturesque—world of powerful currents and tides, submerged remnants of the harbor's historic piers, abandoned buoys, and sunken vessels.

The harbor has at least three levels. Just below the surface are half-sunken logs and pilings from the harbor's ancient piers, along with abandoned fishing and mooring lines. Going deeper, there are powerful tidal currents that influence every vessel in the harbor, and half-submerged, abandoned skiffs and small boats that are dangers to navigation. Sitting on the murky bottom are abandoned lobster pots, sunken boats, and even used tires and shopping carts that have been thrown off the docks. Finally, buried deep in the muck of almost 400 years are the remnants of traditional sailing vessels, antique anchors from clipper ships, and large quantities of oil and grease that have been pumped from the bilges of countless fishing boats. As our writing team contemplated Gloucester harbor and thought about the complicated world below the surface, insights and connections emerged.

Insight #1. The first insight was that the enactment of the Common Theory assumes a clear, straightforward journey as educators cross from one side of the harbor to the other. The Common Theory is clear, straightforward, and uncomplicated (hopefully) as it goes from schools *as they currently are* on one side of the harbor to *reformed schools* on the other.

Insight #2. The Common Theory of school reform assumes educators have light sailing, fair winds, and a clear direction to improved, reformed schools. However, like Cathy and Michael, most educators find that the journey from schools *as they are* to *improved schools* does not happen in a calm harbor, but in the much more unstable, risky, and complicated environment under the surface. Unlike the fair sailing presumed by the Common Theory, the depths of the harbor of school improvement are full of taken-for-granted assumptions, habitual ways of working, and messy, below-the-surface complications that characterize real schools.

This complicated harbor of school improvement is pictured in Figure 1.2.

As Cathy and Michael discovered, in real schools the actual path to school improvement requires us to dive into complicated waters filled with hidden rules, competing commitments, and, in many cases, an organizational culture characterized by "conservatism, isolationism, and presentism" (Hargreaves & Shirley, 2009, p. 2505; see also Lortie, 1975).

Insight #3. Systemic school reform often seems elusive for the adherents of the Common Theory simply because it takes little account of the unseen forces and obstacles of the "harbor" in which the theory is enacted. It ignores that schools are built upon traditions and deeply held norms. Schools are run by leaders and powered by teachers, all of whom hold a range of different, and even competing, assumptions about teaching and learning, and are at very different stages of their careers. Schools operate in community contexts that are often complicated and contentious. Real change takes place in the deeper, murky waters of the harbor.

Understanding the Murky Depths

One useful way to understand the murky depths of the harbor of school improvement is to use the lens of organizational culture. Edgar Schein, a foundational theorist on this topic, suggests that culture can also be charted by depth (Schein, 2016).

Just a few feet below the surface of the water are the "visible artifacts," the organizational structures and processes that can be seen by any observer (Schein, 2016). Visible artifacts would include the school building itself, trophies and student artwork in the school lobby, teachers, classroom walls, and organizational structures such as the master schedule.

Halfway down into the depths of the harbor are what Schein (2016) calls the "espoused theories." Espoused theories are what we *say* we do, but they are not always what we actually enact. Mission and vision statements are espoused theories. Many schools have mission statements describing how all students will learn at high levels. Yet many schools with well-intentioned espoused theories still do not provide each student with a high-quality curriculum or expert instruction. Schools and districts proclaim that they will "identify–select–provide–implement–hold accountable–measure" as they move across the harbor of school improvement, but what really happens in their schools is often quite different.

At the deepest depths of the harbor lie an organization's "basic underlying assumptions." These are the unconscious, unexamined, and taken-for-granted values, assumptions, perceptions, and feelings that are the real guides to action in any organization (Schein, 2016). These fundamental assumptions determine how organizations think about power,

Figure 1.2. The Harbor of School Improvement

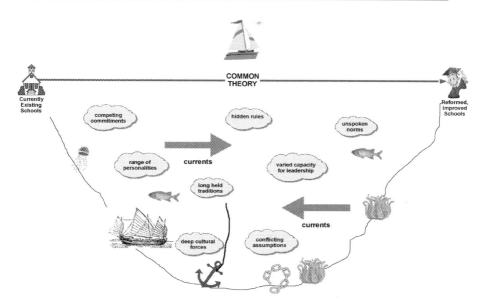

time, space, curriculum, instruction, learning, families, and students. These assumptions lie at the deepest, most invisible part of the harbor. Figure 1.3 describes the depths of the harbor of school improvement as seen through Schein's lens of organizational culture.

Viewing the depths of school reform through an organizational culture lens suggests that the Common Theory will likely be most productive only when it is applied to tasks at the surface. The Common Theory can be used to select a new textbook, move classrooms, tweak the recess schedule, or update curriculum. The real challenge comes when schools dive into the water and attempt to enact broader, deeper changes.

In the case of North Reading Middle School, Cathy and Michael not only wanted to *adopt* MTSS, but they also expected teachers to *reinvent* some of their fundamental assumptions about teaching and learning. Cathy and Michael were hoping to dive a lot deeper into the water than they or the teachers initially were prepared for. They thought that the Common Theory would get them to that *deeper dive* as soon as they identified the need and offered professional development. They were wrong. As we explained earlier, identifying the need was not enough, nor was offering professional development. A deep dive, down past the visible artifacts and espoused theories, all the way to basic underlying assumptions, did not happen. Cathy and Michael needed a different theory of action—an *UnCommon Theory*.

Figure 1.3. An Organizational Culture View of the Harbor of School Improvement

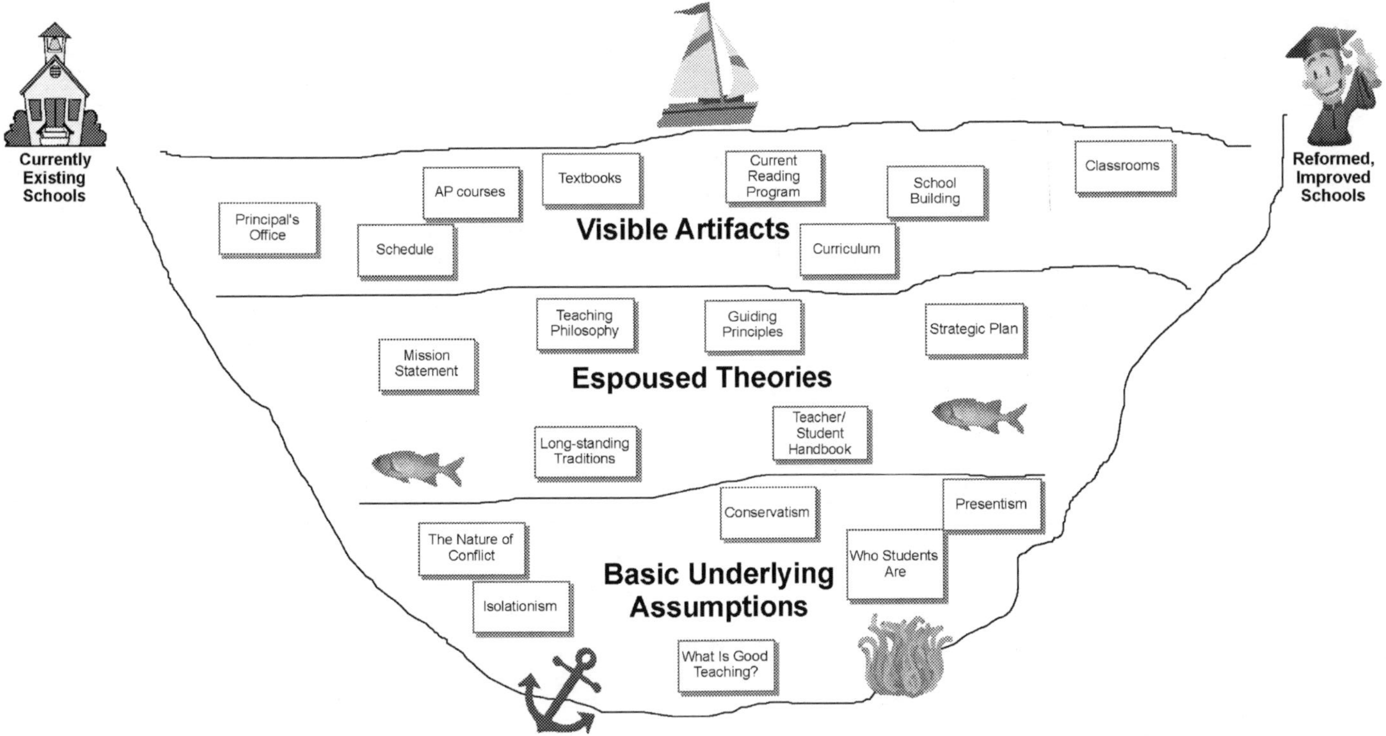

Reformed, Improved Schools

Currently Existing Schools

Visible Artifacts

Classrooms
School Building
Curriculum
Current Reading Program
Textbooks
AP courses
Schedule
Principal's Office

Espoused Theories

Strategic Plan
Guiding Principles
Teacher/ Student Handbook
Teaching Philosophy
Long-standing Traditions
Mission Statement

Basic Underlying Assumptions

Presentism
Who Students Are
Conservatism
What Is Good Teaching?
The Nature of Conflict
Isolationism

WHAT THIS BOOK IS ABOUT:
AN UNCOMMON THEORY OF SCHOOL CHANGE

This book is about an UnCommon Theory of school change. It acknowledges that the Common Theory can be useful as educators make changes that are closest to the surface, changes to the visible artifacts that include school buildings, classrooms, and textbooks. However, deeper changes, long-term improvement, fundamental reform, and, more specifically, the reinvention of schools cannot be done at the level of visible artifacts or espoused theories. These challenges demand surfacing, exploring, and often reinventing deeper fundamental assumptions about teaching, learning, students, and the purpose of schools (McDonald, 2014; McDonald et al., 2018).

The Common Theory is designed to move educators from one side of the harbor of reform to the other as quickly and efficiently as possible. It assumes that school improvement is an easy sail and ignores the competing assumptions, hidden rules, and deeply ingrained habits that are characteristic of most schools. It is these invisible factors that block the well-intentioned reform efforts of educators who rely solely on the Common Theory. In contrast, our UnCommon Theory is based on the *deep dive* that develops educators' collective capacity to investigate hidden assumptions, to withstand the pressure that the dive creates, and to learn how to feel the presence of the emerging future of a school, even when the future cannot be clearly seen.

Stories of the UnCommon Theory

Each chapter in this book is built around the stories of school leaders who have accepted the challenge of examining and reinventing fundamental assumptions and long-held practices. For example, in Chapters 5 and 6, Cathy O'Connell questions inequitable student grouping routines. She began a process called North Reading Middle School 2.0 that led to the reinvention of longstanding practices. Similarly, Matt Underwood from the Atlanta Neighborhood Charter School challenged himself and his school to reinvent inequitable admissions procedures.

These leadership stories are diverse. The stories come from New England, Georgia, and Texas. They are all set in public schools, with stories from urban, suburban, and rural neighborhood and charter schools. The leaders are diverse in terms of age, gender, ethnicity, and role. What these stories have in common is that the leaders

> At the very core, in my belly, it's not equitable. Students weren't given an equal opportunity to learn at a high level. They weren't given an equal opportunity for high-level instruction.
>
> —*Cathy O'Connell*

all had the courage to examine closely held practices and beliefs and find ways to reinvent them.

Each of the stories has successes as well as setbacks; each of the stories is ongoing and incomplete. Unlike the implementation of new initiatives or programs, the work of reinventing fundamental assumptions and practices is never linear, always messy, and requires persistence. In some of our stories, schools were able to successfully surface from the deep dive and reinvent difficult and problematic aspects of their practice. Other schools had to make compromises and are still struggling with big questions, while still others find themselves continuing to build the capacity for reinvention. Notably, they all persist in their commitment to the work of reinventing schools for the benefit of each and every student.

The thread tying each of the stories and leaders together is the personal nature of the work. All the leaders accepted a moral imperative to not just manage their schools, not just improve them, but to unearth bedrock practices and reinvent them. The predictive value of race, class, and gender bothered these leaders. Thus they each accepted a challenge to reinvent their school, a commitment that they could have avoided by sticking with the Common Theory.

How This Book Is Organized

At the heart of this book are the stories of nine educational leaders (principals, school heads, and teacher leaders) who are navigating their own deep dives into school reinvention nationwide. From 2015 to 2017, these stories were collected and crafted iteratively, starting with a series of interviews during which each of us as authors repeatedly observed and talked with the leaders and then made collective sense of the various deep dives. These stories are coupled with our own experiences as principals, facilitators, coaches, teachers, and administrators and serve to illuminate the messy, challenging, and necessary work of following an UnCommon path. Finally, we locate these professional experiences within relevant research and theory to provide a more full-bodied and nuanced portrait of leading for change. This is a book for every educator, parent, or policymaker who already suspects that the Common Theory will never produce the fundamental reinvention of schools that each and every one of our children deserves.

The first two chapters of the book introduce relevant research and theory on school change, adult development, and transformational learning. The next six

> I had to check my moral compass. That's why I knew I had to do something. It wasn't a question of "if." It was a question of how and when, and how could I do it in a way that would build rather than betray trust in the community.
>
> —Jed Lippard

chapters of the book are organized in pairs reflecting the three broad phases of the deep dive. The first chapter of each pair shares the stories of school leaders who are immersed in their own deep dives as well as a theoretical lens to better understand those stories. The second chapter of each pair is more practical and shares the tools and strategies that the leaders used to navigate their deep dives.

The first of the three pairs (Chapters 3 and 4) discusses how formal and informal leaders can learn to observe and understand the complex, contradictory, and often confounding deep water in which school reinvention takes place. The second of the three pairs (Chapters 5 and 6) takes a close look at the turning point of the deep dive, the place where schools and leaders embrace a new future that they sense but might not fully understand or be able to articulate. The third pair (Chapters 7 and 8) is devoted to the ways in which schools enact new practices, structures, or ways of being that the deep dive has produced. To provide a holistic picture of one dive, we recount the story of Andres Lopez, a teacher leader in Stevens High School in San Antonio, Texas, across these chapters and the three phases of the deep dive as a series of text boxes, beginning in Chapter 3.

Finally, in Chapter 9 we discuss not only the opportunities that the UnCommon Theory presents but also the dangers, risks, and challenges that emerge when going against the grain of the Common Theory.

Many Ingredients with No Single Recipe

We want to emphasize that this book is not simply a more complicated, detailed version of the current Common Theory. It is not a step-by-step manual. Rather, it questions whether such a manual or recipe is even possible or useful. Instead, this book introduces essential ingredients necessary to reinvent schools and dive deeper into the issues that challenge teachers and students. This book invites readers to come to their own understanding of what it takes for school reinvention to happen in their own context—with their own students, in their own communities, in their own leadership practice. Each chapter offers stories, strategies, research, theory, tools, and suggestions as ingredients for navigating the deep dive of school reinvention. Yet the ultimate lesson is that individual educators need to write their own recipe; they each need to develop the intentionality, courage, and skill to engage in the ambiguous, uncertain, and even dangerous process that reinventing schools requires. But they also need a list of high-quality ingredients and all the help they can get.

CHAPTER 2

The Deep Dive
An UnCommon Theory

We create programs, we create programs, we create programs.

—Deborah Holman

Deborah Holman, former headmaster of Brookline High School, began the 2015–2016 school year wondering about how to help the school build its capacity for deeper, more challenging work. This was the beginning of her 4th year as headmaster of Brookline High School, a resource-rich school of roughly 1,900 students. Neighboring Boston, Brookline High has regularly topped the charts of successful public high schools in Massachusetts and the nation. Yet Deb wondered "whether all the ways the school has done things in the past—and done them very well—will continue to serve well an increasingly diverse and complex student population as they enter a rapidly changing and largely unknown world."

WHERE THE COMMON THEORY ENDS
AND THE UNCOMMON THEORY BEGINS

At an early fall meeting of the school's Academic Standards Committee, Deb shared her wonderings about the limitations of the Common Theory and the possibility of replacing it with a messier, but perhaps more productive, UnCommon Theory.

> Around here, the theory of action for the last 10 years has centered on the visible/structural level. We create programs, we create programs, we create programs—all good programs that we are not getting rid of. But do we need *more* programs to move forward? Or something deeper, more challenging?

In asking this question, Deb highlights the central tension between the Common and UnCommon Theories.

The Common Theory, which is all about finding the *right* program or initiative, is familiar and safe. Politicians, educators, and parents alike sanction it. Many schools and districts are skilled in implementing the Common Theory. In contrast, the UnCommon Theory asks educators to give up work that is very familiar and in which they are often very skilled, and take up work that is unfamiliar, and in which they are all decidedly unskilled. Deb was asking the school to give up the smooth sailing assumed by the Common Theory for an UnCommon Theory that suggested a deep dive into the murky waters of school reinvention. None of this is easy work.

CHALLENGING THE COMMON THEORY AND "SOLUTIONITIS"

Deb's question surfaces what Anthony Bryk (2015) calls "solutionitis." Bryk explains, "When a pressing problem presents itself, we often jump to implement a policy or programmatic change before fully understanding the exact problem to be solved. We call this phenomena solutionitis" (p. 468). Bryk argues that the pressure from the Common Theory to implement new programs, craft new policies, and carry out new initiatives is powerful and hard to resist:

> By seeing complex matters through a narrow lens, solutionitis often lures decision makers into unproductive strategies. With educational institutions under constant scrutiny, coupled with urgency for change, educators have become an easy target for such "solutions" to move quickly across our field. We become disappointed when promised positive results do not readily emerge, and then we just move on to the next new idea. (p. 468)

Bryk is suspicious of how the Common Theory encourages "seeing complex matters through a narrow lens." Both Deb Holman and Bryk are arguing for a new paradigm, a deep dive into the murky depths of the harbor of school reinvention where "the complexity is real, and it cannot be sidestepped by standardizing all activity in an effort to 'teacher-proof' instructional environments" (Bryk, 2015, p. 474). Yet, as Deb says, a deep dive into all this complexity is "just tougher."

THE UNCOMMON THEORY:
EXPLORING THE DEEP DIVE IN SCHOOLS

The challenge of the deep dive is that the outcome is largely unknown. The future has yet to emerge. It needs to be invented and cannot be implemented in the same ways that schools adopt textbooks or change the bus schedule. The deep dive is risky and demands much from leaders, teachers, and the school community. The deep dive is not about school improvement, new initiatives, or the latest programs; it is about accepting the challenge of ensuring that the high-level skills and competencies demanded by the 21st century are available to each and every one of the students. It is about reinvention.

The unknown future of the deep dive offers a particularly daunting challenge for schools and school leaders who feel a sense of urgency around the inadequacy of our educational system to serve well each and every child. Many educators feel both a profound urgency for reinventing a system based on inequitable educational practice and a sense of dread that diving into the deep harbor of organizational culture, school politics, hidden agendas, and competing assumptions entails. Neither the urgency nor the risks should be minimized.

The UnCommon Theory is hardly without precedent. Movements such as those led by the Coalition of Essential Schools (Sizer, 2004), Big Picture Schools (Littky, 2004), and Expeditionary Learning (Cousins, 2000) have challenged the linear, mechanistic thinking of the Common Theory, and offered deeper, more egalitarian, student-centered conceptualizations of education. Various theorists such as Seymour Sarason (1996), Larry Cuban (2003), John Goodlad (2004), and Ted Sizer (2004) have argued for a more authentic, democratic, equitable vision of schools based not on models but on principles. Yet, despite all of this good work, the Common Theory thrives.

Understanding the Deep Dive

The social change theorist Otto Scharmer (2009) offers a useful framework for understanding the complexities, and vagaries, of the deep dive. The essential question for Scharmer's work—and ours—is: "What is required in order to learn and act from the future as it emerges?" (p. 14). In other words, how do leaders meet the most daunting challenges such as those connected to race, privilege, power, and the reinvention of schools when there is no program to buy, textbook to adopt, or initiative to implement—that is, when the Common Theory just does not apply?

Scharmer proposes that deep change happens in three phases:

1. Observing and understanding the present
2. Turning toward an emerging future
3. Enacting the new future

The first phase is observation and understanding. Seeing what is happening in any organization is challenging because we tend to *see* only those assumptions that the organization already supports. Scharmer (2009) describes how we typically "download the patterns of the past" (p. 39). For example, it is hard to imagine a school whose schedule is not divided into content-specific blocks of time controlled by individual teachers working with students of certain ages (and abilities). Yet, once this "downloaded pattern of the past" is identified, it can be seen with fresh eyes and perhaps even suspended so that other possibilities might emerge. As a result, the organization might begin to see different possibilities and even begin to sense a different future. Chapters 3 and 4 discuss how leaders learn to observe and use what they see to help their organizations understand and escape the downloaded patterns of the past.

Scharmer's second phase is what we call the turning point of the deep dive. The key elements of the first phase—observation, suspending our assumptions, looking at the organization with fresh eyes, and seeing emerging possibilities—are important steps in any deep change effort, but they are not action. Observation needs to be turned into action. Scharmer (2009) calls this second phase of the deep dive "presencing." This is the turning point when the leader and the organization feel that the emerging future is so close that it cannot be avoided. At this point, the organization can see the shortcomings of the downloaded patterns. However, during this phase the organization also feels unstable, teetering between the known but less satisfactory past and the hopeful but uncertain future. How leaders navigate the turning point of the deep dive is discussed in Chapters 5 and 6.

The third phase completes the turn toward a new future. Scharmer (2009) says that in this phase the organization crystallizes a new vision, prototypes the new future, and finally embodies the new future in new practices and structures. During this phase the emerging future becomes real. It is reminiscent of the Common Theory except that the Common Theory takes place without the deep dive into and investigation of the assumptions, hidden rules, and downloaded patterns of the organization. Chapters 7 and 8 discuss how leaders emerge from the deep dive and institutionalize the emerging future. Figure 2.1 summarizes the three phases of the deep dive.

Leading the Deep Dive

As explained in Chapter 1, the Common Theory asks leaders to follow a recipe—identify a need, choose a program or initiative, provide some professional learning, hold teachers accountable, and measure results. The goals—the adoption of a new math textbook or block schedule—are clear, and a thoughtful implementation of the Common Theory can often improve an aspect of teachers' practice.

The deep dive of the UnCommon Theory is more challenging because the results are not often clear, and the goal is not the improvement of a

Figure 2.1. The Three Phases of the Deep Dive

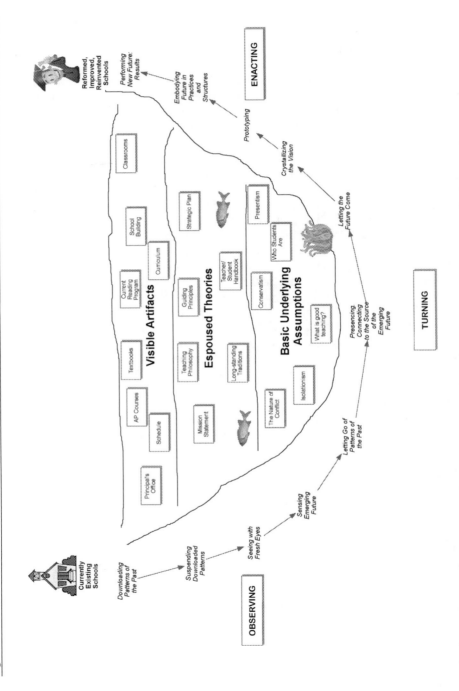

known practice, but the questioning and rethinking of assumptions that support the existing practice in order to create a fundamentally new practice. The goal is not improvement, but *reinvention*. In general, the UnCommon Theory is more challenging than the Common Theory in three ways.

First, the goals of the deep dive are daunting. The deep dive is not about perfecting what educators already do in schools, but rather about challenging and reinventing the status quo. It is about replacing current practice with a more justified, equitable, better practice—the reinvention of schools. This is risky leadership work.

Second, the deep dive invariably surfaces and disturbs the deep assumptions upon which schools are built. Because organizational culture is invisible and shared deeply, the Common Theory cannot change it. A different organizational culture cannot be adopted like a student handbook or implemented like a new vocabulary program. Changing culture demands a new leadership practice.

Third, both adult *learning* and *development* are required. Adult *learning* is necessary when educators implement the district's new math program or literacy initiative. The Common Theory requires adult learning. However, reinventing practice, rethinking the purpose of schools, replacing the unproductive relationships that characterize some of our schools requires that adults develop the capacity to work collaboratively and be reflective. The reinvention of schools requires that adults consider demanding questions and become comfortable with the fact that there are no easy answers. The deep dive requires adults who can see conflict as a necessary part of organizational and professional growth, can speak their own truths, and expect that others will speak their own (and often very different) truths.

Supporting the Deep Dive

In a meeting with her administrative team, Deb Holman described a collaborative exploration that the high school needed to embark on in order to better serve its growing, changing population of students. "What I see, and have been saying to people, is that we are now beginning a deep dive into some stuff that is tougher, and really about adults, a lot more about adults, instruction, and school culture." The three big ideas in Deb's conceptualization of the emerging work at Brookline High School also drive the reinvention of schools *and* this book. They are the following:

1. *The deep dive is "really about adults, a lot more about adults."* At the heart of the deep dive is adult development. The deep dive demands not only that adults learn new skills, but that they also develop the capacity to rethink fundamental assumptions about schools, teaching, students, and even what it means to be an

educator. Adult development builds capacity to manage the anxiety produced by questions that have no easy answers, readily
available models, or prepackaged programs.
2. *The deep dive is about uncovering, managing, and reinventing "culture."*
   Organizational culture is difficult to see because we are immersed
   in it. Culture is even harder to change because it is comprised of
   layers of programs, practices, ideas, rituals, customs, and ways of
   doing things that at one time served the organization well, but
   perhaps not as well now, and perhaps not at all in the future.
3. *The deep dive is indeed "tougher" than the business-as-usual enactment of
   the Common Theory.* The need for the deep dive is based on a conviction that the Common Theory—responding to organizational
   challenges by creating more and more programs and initiatives—
   no longer works. However, the deep dive is riskier and more un-
   predictable than the Common Theory, and understandably raises
   the anxiety of teachers, leaders, and community members.

The Deep Dive Is "Really About Adults." Educators are continually asked to
learn. They learn new literacy strategies, classroom community-building
techniques, time-management systems, and how to work on teams. The
list of things educators are expected to learn—because of the power of the
Common Theory—is long. Many theorists would call this type of learning
informational (Mezirow, 2000). Informational learning changes what we
know, increases our content knowledge, or provides us with new skills. Informational learning is typically the result of the professional development
associated with the Common Theory. Although informational learning is,
by any account, a good thing, significant research suggests that the professional development that supports it has, at best, mixed results (Guskey &
Yoon, 2009).

Learning theory suggests that there is another type of adult learning:
learning that is transformational. Transformational learning (or transformative learning) is different from informational learning. It is learning
that changes not only what we know, but also *how* we know what we
know, and even who we are and how we respond to the world. Mezirow
(2000) explains:

> Transformative learning refers to the process by which we transform
> our taken-for-granted references (meaning perspectives, habits of mind,
> mind-sets) to make them more inclusive, discriminating, open emotion-
> ally, capable of change, and reflective so that they may generate beliefs
> and opinions that will prove more true or justified to guide action. (p. 7)

Informational-learning experiences can be very valuable, but while
they might improve our practice, they do not help us surface or question

the hidden assumptions underneath that practice. It is only when a learning experience is pulled toward the transformational end of the continuum that the possibility of surfacing, questioning, and challenging fundamental assumptions arises. Transformational learning builds organizational capacity for successive deep dives into the hidden assumptions upon which our schools and teaching practices are built.

In Chapters 3 and 4 on the observing phase of the deep dive, we describe how constructive-developmental theory (Kegan, 1998) helps educators understand the connections between building the capacity to see and challenge deeply held assumptions, transformational learning, and the work of deep cultural change.

The Deep Dive Is "About Culture." The literature on school change calls the fundamental assumptions, commitments, and traditions that make up the complicated waters of our harbor of school improvement *organizational culture,* as we introduced in Chapter 1. Schein (2016) defines organizational culture as ". . .the accumulated shared learning of that group as it solves its problems of external adaptation and internal integration; which has worked well enough to be considered valid and, therefore, to be taught to new members as the correct way to perceive, think, feel, and behave in relation to those problems" (p. 6). Organizational culture manifests itself and can be analyzed in three ways—or layers—visible artifacts, espoused values, and fundamental assumptions (Schein, 2016). All schools have organizational cultures that have very little to do with how folks get along or whether or not they like each other. Three elements of Schein's definition are worth highlighting: Organizational cultures are (1) shared, (2) learned, and (3) at some point in time worked well.

We will explore the implications of organizational culture in the second, or turning, phase of the deep dive (Chapters 5 and 6). However, it might be important to note that because culture is shared, learned, and worked well, it cannot be reinvented using the tools of the Common Theory. It is not possible to purchase a new culture the way a school might purchase science kits. Nor can a school implement a new culture the way that a school might implement a schedule change. The deep dive demands a different leadership practice.

The Deep Dive Is Not "Business as Usual." In general, the literature on school change makes an important distinction between the *improvement* of schools and the *reinvention* of schools. The essential point is that *improving* schools and *reinventing* schools are two very different tasks that place different learning demands on the adults who are asked to carry them out.

School improvement can be accomplished, for example, by adopting a new curriculum or implementing extended learning time. It is in the realm of school improvement that the Common Theory makes the most sense. School improvement often leans toward what various theorists call "technical" (Heifetz, 1994), "Discourse I" (Eubanks, Parish, & Smith, 1997), or "first order" (Cuban & Usdan, 2002) approaches. The list of improvements schools regularly adopt is long and varied; teaching phonemic awareness, wearing uniforms, single-sex classrooms, and expanded Advanced Placement programs are just a few examples. Most of these improvements are research-based, and all can help make schools better places for students. Each one has advocates. However, each of these changes could be considered "technical" or "first order" because they do not necessarily require fundamental shifts in the way adults in schools think about and enact their work.

School *reinvention* is different. The reinvention of schools requires a deep dive into school culture. Reinvention has been called "adaptive" (Heifetz, Grashow, & Linsky, 2009), "Discourse II" (Eubanks et al., 1997), or "second order" (Cuban & Usdan, 2002) work. School reinvention asks educators not only to adopt a new program or approach, but also to rethink what it means to be a teacher and to challenge assumptions about schools, practice, and students. School reinvention requires a higher order of adult development because it asks educators to think in complex ways about who students are, how students are grouped for instruction, how schools choose to use time, or what it means to be an educator committed to equitable teaching practice. We will dig more deeply into the distinction between the improvement and reinvention of schools in Chapters 7 and 8.

THEORY AND PRACTICE: THE DEEP DIVE IN CONTEXT

This book exists at the intersection of theory and practice. It takes seriously the voices of practitioners like Deb Holman and Cathy O'Connell. It understands that practice is always context-specific and that context accounts for much of the complexity in educator practice. For example, where the school is located, who the students are, how the district is organized and funded, and how leaders are chosen — each makes an important difference in teacher, leadership, and organizational practice. It is important to understand that each deep dive takes place in a particular context and for a particular period of time.

Our initial conceptualization of the deep dive (refer to Figure 2.1) suggests that all deep dives are similar in that they are a process by which an organization observes, understands, and shifts the fundamental assumptions upon which it is built. A simplified version of the deep dive might look like Figure 2.2.

Figure 2.2. A Simplified Version of the Deep Dive

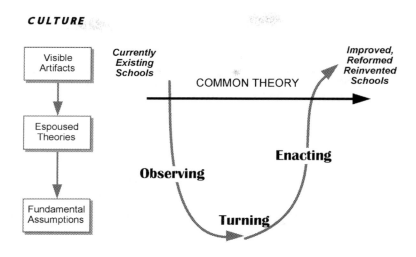

In this context-free conceptualization, the deep dive delves into the most fundamental assumptions upon which a school is built. Yet schools are not context free. Schools are situated in complex environments. Factors such as economic resources, political realities, school and district leadership, teacher capacity, community relationships, and public policy have a powerful influence on schools and the degree of reform they can undertake (McDonald, 2014; McDonald et al., 2018). In many cases, the depth of the deep dive, especially the first dive a leader and school take together, might be fairly shallow and only lightly touch on fundamental assumptions. Contextual factors will always influence the depth of a dive. The depth of the dive is influenced by the school context in which the dive is situated, including the capacity, skill, and courage of the school leader. Simply put, the deepest dive might not always be possible at any given moment in time, due to a variety of contextual factors. However, a shallow dive can be a critical step in the work of transforming schools. Shallow dives help build a leader's and an organization's capacity to dive deeper "next time." Given this, it might be best to view deep dives as iterative by nature, taking place over time, and growing successively deeper.

DEEP DIVES OVER TIME

If, for example, a leader and school take a "shallow" dive into scheduling practices, they might touch on issues of how time is used and who benefits

Figure 2.3. A Shallow Dive Preceding a Deep Dive

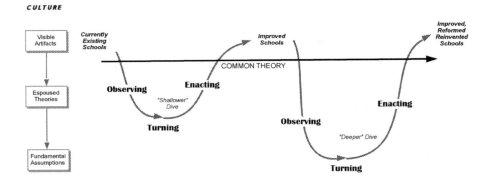

(and who does not) from the status quo. The school desperately needs a new schedule for the next year, and this contextual element alone means that the observing, turning, and enacting phases of the deep dive will be limited. The school needs a new schedule and students will arrive in the fall—no matter what. The dive might not go as deep as it could.

In the fall, after students have arrived and the new schedule has been enacted, the school might build on what was learned about observing, turning, and enacting, and dive into how students are grouped for instruction. In this second iteration of the dive, the school may very well dive deeper into questions of what it means to be smart, who has ability, and who makes these determinations. The school might dive into who benefits from current instructional practices and who does not. If the school has developed enough capacity, it might even dive into how these questions connect to issues of race, language, and equity. Figure 2.3 illustrates this scenario.

There is no "correct" depth for a deep dive because each dive is limited and shaped by a myriad of contextual factors. However, the experience of seeing beyond the visible artifacts of a school into its fundamental assumptions helps a school learn the skills of observing, turning, and enacting. Like all learning, it builds upon itself.

To further complicate matters, because schools work over long periods of time, it is easy to imagine even more complicated conceptualizations of the deep dive. For example, School A, which has some experience with both shallow and deep dives, might experience a financial disaster, or a drastic change in leadership, or a public policy that affects the school. Such circumstances might cause the school to completely abandon any attempt at a deep dive for a period of time. In contrast, School B, which has less experience with deep dives, might receive a sudden infusion of resources or experience a change in leadership that unexpectedly supports

Figure 2.4. How School Context Affects Dives: School A

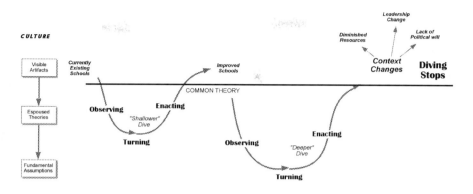

Figure 2.5. How School Context Affects Dives: School B

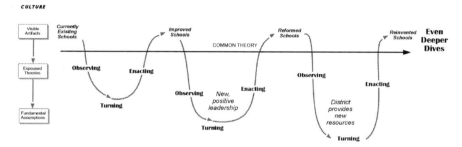

deep dives. The dives of both these schools are illustrated in Figure 2.4 (School A) and 2.5 (School B).

Finally, organizational theory (Lewin, 1947; Schein, 2016) suggests that there might be a long period of enactment, or long periods of relative stability between dives. Any deep dive uses significant capacity, political will, and energy, and a school might need a period of time to replenish itself, as illustrated in Figure 2.6.

In summary, there are three broad implications related to the fact that deep dives are iterative and take place in complicated contexts. First, dives can be of different depths. Schools are situated in vastly different contexts, and a school's particular context can support or limit the depth of the dive. Second, over time a school can participate in many deep dives. As schools learn about observing, turning, and enacting, they build capacity for deeper dives. Yet context (e.g., leadership changes, lack of political will, financial crisis) can also limit a school's capacity to undertake any deep dive. Third, a school often requires a period of stability between

Figure 2.6. Period of Stability Between Deep Dives

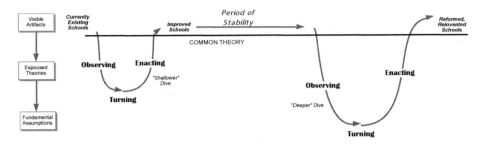

deep dives. Schools, despite some rhetoric to the contrary, cannot always function well in environments of continual change at the deepest level.

As explained above, each of the next three pairs of chapters is connected to a particular body of theory and research and to a particular phase of the deep dive. Chapters 3 and 4 describe the observing part of the deep dive using the lens of adult-development theory. Chapters 5 and 6 discuss the turning of the deep dive, especially as it relates to organizational-culture theory. Chapters 7 and 8 examine the enactment phase and its connection to organizational-change theory. All chapters incorporate the stories of courageous leaders engaging their schools in deep dives.

CHAPTER 3

Observing
The First Phase of the Deep Dive

The model of getting principals ready right now is management- and compliance-oriented rather than people- or leadership-oriented. Leaders have to be equipped to understand how to put teachers' strengths to work and how to build capacity in teachers and schools.

—Liz Ozuna

Jed Lippard, the former head of school of the Prospect Hill Academy (PHA) Charter School in Somerville and Cambridge, Massachusetts, describes the first movement of the deep dive as a series of observational, sense-making, and capacity-building activities: "This early part is characterized by kind of feeling around, observing, collecting information, thinking a lot, talking to folks. This is a lot of personal decision making." Having served as the upper school principal and then head of school at PHA, Jed knows that diving into the harbor of school improvement requires preparation. It involves early moves that build a leader's and school's capacity to see patterns of the past in operation and then engage in conversations about letting go of old patterns. Observing and letting go of past patterns are necessary first steps toward later shifts in thinking and practice.

OBSERVING AT PROSPECT HILL ACADEMY

Jed suggests that there are powerful, straightforward early moves leaders can make when beginning a dive. For Prospect Hill Academy, these involved investing in collaborative inquiry and visiting other schools to help gain perspective. As Jed explains, early on in his work as principal, he

demanded and then provided resources for teacher collaboration. Initially, common planning time was a core requirement and professional expectation, then creating the structures inside of that time and space ensured that meaningful work was actually happening, which then evolved into collaborative inquiry.

Jed also supported faculty observing at other schools: "It's powerful when you get outside of your own space and go into other schools." Both collaborative inquiry and site visits allow leaders and teachers to observe their practices and students in a new light. However, Jed is also careful to remind us of the complexity and murkiness of the early days of a deep dive. When Jed shifted roles, moving from upper school principal (grades 7–12) to working as head of school (pre-K–12 across multiple schools), he sensed that he might be embarking on a deep dive into aligning thinking and practices across what he later called a "13-year narrative." Jed describes a necessary and somewhat challenging shift in his own view of the larger organization: "My view, my lens, completely shifted. It wasn't about what's best for the upper school. It was about what's best for the community as a whole. How do we really create a pre-K–12 school?"

During his 5 years as principal, Jed successfully established strong communication and collaboration systems within the upper school. But now he had to take a much larger view of his role. Jed admits, "I didn't give a damn about the lower school when I was the upper school principal. I didn't want to play nice. I didn't care about pre-K–12 alignment. I didn't care about institutional adherence." Suddenly, thrust into the role of head of school, his perspective had to change. He embarked on the work of observing, uncovering, and letting go of assumptions and past practices that kept the lower and upper schools separate.

As Jed began making sense of his new roles and responsibilities, he also began to see the lack of coherence in pre-K–12 teaching, learning, and collaboration. Jed explains that as part of a larger change initiative in the district he "set up systems and structures that ensured horizontal and vertical alignment [across all grades]. I needed to make sure that that was happening institutionally. None of those systems were in place." With a new role and fresh eyes, Jed had to think about how faculty might join in observing, uncovering, and letting go of isolationist tendencies. Jed needed the help of the faculty to make this change a reality. It was essential to bring teachers along with him on a deep dive into creating a more coherent pre-K–12 experience for students.

OBSERVING AT MATHIS HIGH SCHOOL FOR INTERNATIONAL STUDIES

Liz Ozuna was the founding principal of the Mathis High School for International Studies, a magnet school on a traditional, comprehensive high school campus in Mathis, a small town south of San Antonio, Texas. When she was hired, she was tasked with starting a small, internationally themed magnet school aligned with a national network of schools, the Asia Society's (2018) International Studies Schools Network (ISSN). Liz had served in a leadership position in an ISSN school in San Antonio. The superintendent knew of Liz's work there; he and the school board were eager to bring this global studies innovation to their town.

Although Liz had been in leadership positions previously, this was her first principalship. The superintendent and school board wanted the school launched quickly, even though they knew the ISSN framework was quite different and new. Liz was hired in April and tasked with opening the school in August with its first class of students, the 9th grade. She moved to Mathis in May and began hiring teachers, including from the existing high school, who were interested in the new school concept as well as teachers new to Mathis; she also had to recruit students for the school. Liz and the faculty formally began together in June, with the better part of June and July to plan for the school's opening and first year. There was a lot of hesitation and concern from the community and from teachers at the existing school who saw this as a competing interest. Liz knew she was beginning a deep dive that would challenge assumptions and practices. It became a question of how to begin and how deep she should—or could—go.

New to Mathis, Liz began meeting the teachers, students, district, and community. The new school would be located on the campus of the existing school, so she had to get to know the existing school's culture as she shaped the new one, including the international studies focus. And in such a small town and district—with one elementary, middle, and high school—she had to simultaneously figure out prevalent patterns and assumptions across the schools and district—what people called "the Mathis way."

Liz recounts that community members asked questions like, "Why are you teaching Chinese in Mathis?" She created opportunities for dialogue with families by asking questions herself, like "What are your hopes and fears for your child?" Liz discovered that "a fear was that we could not change the culture of our school and our small town to expect kids would be successful." Liz knew she had to ask questions, listen, and observe in every community-based interaction. She was building her knowledge and testing pieces of what would eventually become the story she would tell about the new school to herself, faculty, parents, and the community.

A deep dive takes place over time, not at breakneck pace. It involves collectively gathering data, making sense of that data, and guiding the development of a plan, one that requires understanding the school culture and building capacity for reinvention.

OBSERVING CULTURE, BUILDING CAPACITY, AND MANAGING ANXIETY

In this and the following chapter, the stories of Jed Lippard, Liz Ozuna, and Andres Lopez highlight the complexity of early moves of the deep dive. School leaders and communities must engage in a great deal of learning to collectively see and make meaning of current practices in ways that allow them to step back and ask deeper questions about their work. Through conversations with Jed, Liz, Andres, and the other leaders in this book, we have come to understand that there are three productive ways leaders and schools begin to dive: (1) engaging in observational work; (2) building collective capacity; and (3) managing anxiety. Each of these is described in the following sections.

Observing Culture and Making Sense of Patterns of the Past: Connecting the Dots

Using the Common Theory, leaders might identify an organizational dilemma such as lack of pre-K–12 instructional coherence, select a popular solution such as professional learning communities (PLCs), and move forward as quickly as possible. But as Cathy O'Connell explained in Chapter 1, following such a simple "recipe" is really a recipe for disaster. The Common Theory doesn't fundamentally change teaching and learning, partly because it does not help school members recognize, disrupt, and then replace fundamental norms and prevalent patterns of the past.

The UnCommon Theory suggests that a leader who elects to enter into a deep dive will delay selecting and implementing an intervention. Embarking on a deep dive, leaders begin by observing school culture closely, trying to understand a dilemma or need in the specific context of their organization before introducing new practices, programs, or initiatives. Observing the existing culture and making sense of the past habits of the organization (and its inhabitants) are essential; otherwise, a change effort may be doomed from the start. Importantly, leaders must include and help members of the organization see their own habits and patterns of the past—this cannot be the leader's work alone but is done in collaboration with colleagues. Early collaborative work sets the stage for later "co-enacting" of prototypes (Chapters 7 and 8) that can have long-lasting, far-reaching effects.

Jed describes his early observational and sense-making work as playing the role of the "chief dot connector." Becoming head of school, Jed had to look across the campuses, "see the vision and coherence, and also where things [were] not aligned." He developed "the ability to integrate the various movements" of the complex and somewhat fragmented organization. In his role as dot connector, Jed knew that he needed to support the faculty in observing and making sense of isolated practices.

ANDRES LOPEZ'S STORY 1: OBSERVING

This is the start of Andres Lopez's story, the teacher leader introduced in the Preface. His story will progress across the chapters via text boxes, which are numbered to help track the story's progression. Being new to his school, Andres brought fresh eyes to existing patterns and practices and made them visible to colleagues.

I looked at the approved reading list, and I said, "You know, we don't have a lot of books approved that are novels by women of color." I gave them the number of those books and the total number of books on the book list. I put that out there not as, "This is a problem." I said, "I really want to expand the reading list to include more women of color. I'd love to work with any-body who's got a similar interest." That's an easy thing to point out and say, "Look, there's a gap here. We need to figure this out." Then, guess what? Teachers that were like-minded or had a similar idea, we slowly found each other and made things happen. We started by supplementing the textbook, and then moved to expanding the book list beyond the textbook and tra-ditional book list. I would slowly really try to get in people's heads in a way that wasn't threatening, but that got them to think a little differently about what they do on a daily basis.

Whereas Jed describes himself as the dot connector, Liz describes herself as the "sense maker." "To me, the primary responsibility of the leader is that of the original sense maker—taking all the stuff and putting it together so that it can be understood and get tackled. Sometimes I think that means making some decisions about what is going to be our priority." Like Jed, Liz was observing, finding patterns, making connections, and doing some interpreting with the teachers. Amidst that sense making, Liz was figuring out—and helping the school to figure out—"where the ten-der spots were," as culture consists of habits, practices, and also feelings.

Scharmer (2009) talks about this early "diving" work as observing and making sense of "patterns of the past" (p. 39), or in other words, no-ticing and making sense of habits that are the result of an organization's collective history. As pointed out in Chapter 2, every organization has a particular culture, developed over time to serve the organization (Schein, 2016). However, over time, many processes and habits become outdated and no longer serve the organization's goals, like a closet that continually was filled with new clothes over decades without being cleared out or sorted. This is particularly true in schools where new practices are fre-quently adopted to meet the needs of shifting student populations, rapid changes in standards, increasing use of technology, and so on, all layered on top of one another, without periodic review or culling.

For instance, when Jed operated as the upper school principal, he communicated and interacted directly and frequently with almost every teacher in the school (approximately 30 faculty). However, this communication system no longer served him well when he moved into the role of head of school. Jed explained: "During my tenure as the head of school, we grew from 700 to 1,200 kids, and we had to evolve organizationally, which necessitated a shift in my leadership. I couldn't be everywhere all the time." The old patterns of faculty–leadership communication needed to change, and Jed's own reliance on being involved in all decisions would no longer serve the organization well. Observing these previous patterns of communication and decisionmaking, and noticing that they were no longer serving the organization well, was one of the first moves in the school's deep dive focused on building pre-K–12 coherence.

In order to see with "fresh eyes" (Scharmer, 2009, p. 22), educators must engage in a great deal of observation, listening, and capacity-building so new conversations and opportunities can emerge. Ideally, as leaders are doing the early work of the dive, they are observing and listening in ways that help the leader understand more clearly the nature of any dilemma, but also build the capacity of the entire organization to observe and understand past patterns.

If done well, the early observational work of the deep dive can build shared language and structures that support slower, deeper thinking and subvert the knee-jerk responses of the Common Theory. We expand on the particular moves that support this initial phase of the deep dive in Chapter 4. However, before turning to strategies, it is important to understand the next big frame that supports initial diving work.

Building Capacity by Attending to Adult Development

In addition to describing himself as the "dot connector," Jed also names an equal if not more important role that leaders play at this stage: "chief adult developer." Jed put it this way: "For my own leadership, I don't know if I could function without some knowledge of adult developmental theory, having some knowledge of the fact that adults make meaning in qualitatively different ways. I don't know how I could do this job without that. As chief adult developer, I'm trying to lead from a place of developmental intention."

In order to lead the reinvention of schooling, a school leader must understand and frame school reform as a challenge not just of adult *learning*, but as a matter of adult *development*. This is a challenge that UnCommon leaders must tackle head-on, positioning themselves as both lead learner and adult developer.

Jed tries to "lead from a place of developmental intention" and "hold people in relationship." To Jed, this means supporting school faculty, staff, and other leaders as they grow their capacity to understand and collaboratively address teaching and learning dilemmas. In order to successfully engage in a deep dive, both the leader and the faculty in a school must have the capacity to step back from business as usual, look at their own work and habits with fresh eyes, and prepare to make the leap into doing work in new, and therefore potentially uncomfortable, ways.

The Common Theory presumes that adults in schools can simply learn a new set of strategies, processes, and habits. However, the Un-Common Theory reveals that deeper changes in schools are not the result of merely learning something new, something else, or something more. Deep change is a matter of shifting mindsets, paradigms, and assumptions—deeper shifts that require more than adult *learning*. Consequently, true school reinvention is the result of adult *development*, with the entire school community developing new capacities for seeing and understanding complex dilemmas, staying in difficult conversations, and reframing current assumptions.

For Jed, some of his growth in moving into the role of head of school was letting go of ownership of the upper school. He had to step back from that role and from his close management of a smaller group of faculty. Jed explains:

> The minute that I became the head of school, I intentionally moved out of the upper school building and went to the lower school, where I wasn't the most popular person. I didn't know that much about elementary education. People didn't know me, and I didn't know them. My view, my lens completely shifted, and it wasn't about what's best for the upper school. It was about what's best for the community as a whole.

Each of these actions required a shift in identity and capacity for Jed. He found himself in an uncomfortable new position, with the task of letting go of previous roles and ways of working. These moves weren't just physical ones, like moving to a new office, or simply a matter of learning a new role. They reflect deeper, developmental shifts for Jed and the organization. He had to leave his comfort zone by letting go of his own sense of expertise, his familiarity and comfort with leading only secondary school teachers, and his assumptions about natural divides between early and later educational enterprises. Jed had to rethink his identity.

Leading for adult development pushes against the many competing forces in schools today, including Common Theory rhetoric and policies that encourage "solutionitis," as explained in Chapter 2 (Bryk, 2015). Jed describes the tension between being "an adult developer" and being "the boss." While he might wish to support the faculty in becoming more complex thinkers over time, those same community members often expected Jed to maintain his role as "boss," making sure that all of the logistical and management aspects of the leadership role were being fulfilled. Jed acknowledges: "[A leader is] doomed if there's not deliberate, conscious, and intentional work on development." We couldn't agree more.

Constructive Developmental Theory. When Jed mentions the importance of understanding "adult development theory," he is referring to the fundamental tenets of constructive developmental theory (Kegan, 1998):

1. Adults continually work to make sense of their experiences (constructive).
2. The ways that adults make sense of their world can change and grow more complex over time (developmental).
3. Four of the most common ways adults understand their worlds can be described as instrumental, socializing, self-authoring, and self-transformational.

In Kegan's terms, instrumental knowers seek concrete answers and specific processes. They want to know the "right way" to teach guided reading or line kids up for lunch. Socializing knowers, on the other hand, understand that there are many perspectives and multiple right answers. Socializing knowers work well in groups, can be reflective, and even put the needs of the group first. Yet they rely on the group to help evaluate their own actions and system of beliefs; thus, socializing knowers can become quite uncomfortable when they experience conflict with the group. Socializing knowers find it difficult to stand in opposition to the group while still being part of it, whereas self-authoring knowers hold an internal set of standards by which they can evaluate their own actions; they can tolerate ambiguity and even stand in opposition to a group while still remaining part of it. Finally, self-transformational knowers are suspicious of absolutes, including their own internal set of standards.

Furthermore, self-transformational knowers are able to step back from their own internal set of standards and see themselves as always incomplete and growing, embracing differences or otherness as part of themselves. For example, a self-transformative knower is able to simultaneously self-identify as Catholic but also acknowledge and incorporate elements of other religious stances within their own belief system. They embrace conflict because it opens the door to increasingly authentic, useful, and more complex versions of themselves. Table 3.1 summarizes these stages of adult development.

Constructive developmental theory does not consider one way of knowing fundamentally better than another. Instead, constructive developmental theory suggests that individuals at different stages of adult development might experience anxiety or satisfaction depending on the match between the personal and professional tasks at hand and the degree

Table 3.1. Stages of Adult Development and Ways of Knowing

Instrumental Knowers	Socializing Knowers	Self-Authoring Knowers	Self-Transforming Knowers
• Have concrete needs • Believe that rules are important and always search for the "right way" • Are most comfortable with concrete, specific processes • Have limited interest in reflection or collaboration when their own needs are not met	• Focus on others • Believe that group needs are important • Can put a group's needs before their own • Can be collaborative and reflective • Are uncomfortable with conflicting opinions, values, and behaviors	• Are reflective about themselves and their context • Can live with ambiguity • Evaluate their own actions according to internal standards • Expect and accept conflict • Consider their personal goals and ideas as very important • Are able to stand in opposition to a group	• Refuse to see self as a single system • Are suspicious of absolutes • Hold their own ideas and beliefs as tentative, incomplete, and ever-evolving • Welcome conflict as a vehicle for finding more useful, justified answers

Note. Adapted from *Leadership for Powerful Learning* (p. 6), by A. Breidenstein, K. Fahey, C. Glickman, and F. Hensley, 2012, New York, NY: Teachers College Press.

to which an individual is able to learn and act effectively in response; Figure 3.1 summarizes this idea.

In a school, for example, a teacher who is an instrumental knower looking for concrete answers and specific processes to get them right might find it challenging to consider issues of equitable educational practice. The instrumental knower wants to know how to manage the new reading program, correctly prepare students for the state assessment, and efficiently address the achievement gap. Instrumental knowers do not (yet) think in more complicated ways about the purpose of schooling, or issues of race and equity, which are almost always convoluted and paradoxical.

How Constructive Developmental Theory Supports the Deep Dive. It is not hard to see why it is important for leaders to frame a deep dive in terms of adult development (not simply adult learning). To better serve students, educators certainly need to learn new methods, strategies, and practices (the Common Theory). Adult learning and the acquisition of new techniques will always be an important element of school change. However,

Figure 3.1. The Match Between Context and Ways of Knowing

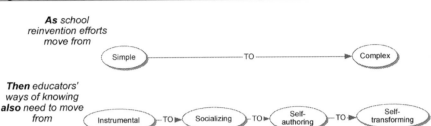

a deep dive necessarily demands adult *development*, for both the leader and the entire community (the UnCommon Theory). For educators to successfully manage the deep dive into the harbor of hidden assumptions, competing commitments, and long-held traditions, they must learn and work in increasingly complicated ways. They have to consider a variety of perspectives, welcome conflict, and live with ambiguity. A deep dive requires both learning new practices, and also questioning long-held and often hidden assumptions, adopting a range of perspectives, living with the anxiety of not knowing, and embracing the conflict that the deep dive engenders. Each of these actions may require adult development. Thus, in order to help reinvent schools, leaders must think and work as chief adult developers. Figure 3.2 summarizes this idea.

Creating Opportunities for Both Individual and Group Development. While constructive developmental theory has long been used to identify and frame the growth and complex thinking of individuals (Kegan, 1998), only recently has it begun to be applied to groups and organizations (Breidenstein et al., 2012; Kegan, Lahey, Miller, Fleming, & Helsing, 2016). When applying constructive developmental theory to groups, it is critical to consider the learning needs of teams and entire organizations, not just the needs of individuals. The stance that a school leader might take changes based on the kinds of learning that entire groups of educators might need to undertake at any particular time. Sometimes a team, or an entire school, might require "instrumental learning . . . where answers, expert knowledge, or technical support are needed" (Breidenstein et al., 2012, p. 9). At other times a team or school might require "socializing learning" where the focus is on "building groups, teams, and schools that are collaborative, reflective, and focused on issues of teaching and learning" (p. 10). At still other times teams or schools might require "self-authoring learning," in which leaders and community members put their own learning on display by "asking difficult questions, by presenting disconfirming data, and by exposing and exploring . . . fundamental assumptions in public" (p. 11). Table 3.2 summarizes four distinct ways in

Figure 3.2. Connecting School Reinvention and Adult Development

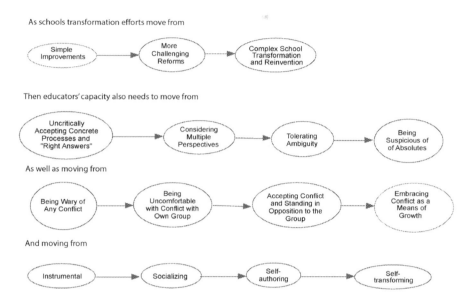

which leaders position themselves as they support groups of adult learners in schools.

Leaders like Jed and Liz understand that when they are beginning to dive into the fundamental assumptions and hidden norms surrounding a particular aspect of schooling, they must adopt the mindset of an adult developer and frame the work of both individuals and groups as adult development work. The act of observing and surfacing hidden norms requires a shift in adult development, an increased capacity of everyone in the community to step back from common practices and examine them more objectively. This move, learning to step back and observe the familiar through a new, critical lens is a matter of adult development (not just adult learning). To build the capacity of community members to engage in this work, leaders sometimes introduce and intentionally use protocols (one of Jed and Liz's major tools, explored further in Chapter 4). Sometimes leaders foster intentional learning communities or develop teacher leadership networks. All of these strategies support adult and professional development.

Without supporting individuals and groups in developing more complex ways of seeing and thinking about their work, there is little hope of ultimately transforming the hidden values and underlying norms of schools. Beginning a deep dive concerned with systemic and structural inequities requires observational and capacity-building work to determine self and group capacity. Questions that leaders might ask themselves include:

Table 3.2 Leadership Stance and School Learning Needs

School Learning Needs	Leadership Stance
Instrumental Learning	Leaders understand issues of teaching and learning; they have considerable knowledge about "best practice" and know how to help teachers find necessary expertise.
Socializing Learning	Leaders understand how to build collaborative groups, support reflective practice, and build school cultures that are focused on issues of teaching and learning.
Self-Authoring Learning	Leaders not only understand instructional issues and how to build reflective, collaborative cultures, but also take an inquiry stance toward their own practice. Leaders become self-authoring learners themselves and promote others' inquiry into their own practice.
Self-Trans-forming Learn-ing	Leaders not only take an inquiry stance toward their own practice, but they understand that their own learning and practice will always be incomplete and is ever-evolving. Leaders become comfortable with incompleteness and ambiguity, both in their own practice and within the organization. Leaders are more able to "let go of" dilemmas that previously held them captive.

Note. Adapted from *Leading for Powerful Learning*, by A. Breidenstein, K. Fahey, C. Glickman, and F. Hensley, 2012, New York, NY: Teachers College Press.

- What kinds of adult development are being exhibited in the school currently (e.g., instrumental, socializing, self-authoring)?
- What kind of learning could be undertaken next, given current ways of thinking and working?
- How might we differentiate adult learning to best support different types of knowers?

In the early parts of the deep dive, leaders are sensing what learning they and the larger group can manage and what small moves might be made to push everyone to think about and see their work in a new light. In Chapter 4 we describe multiple concrete ways in which leaders might act as "chief adult developers."

Adult development necessarily creates anxiety. If educators are working at their growing edges, even with support, there will be challenge. When the work is focused on uncovering and observing culture, the heat turns up even more. Therefore, leaders must learn to manage anxiety within the dive.

ANDRES LOPEZ'S STORY 2: OBSERVING

Being aware that his colleagues were at different places in their learning, Andres began making small moves.

Another time when I "planted a flag" while talking in the teachers' lounge, I said "I can't believe we have Bless Me Ultima in the book room and nobody teaches it. It's the number one selling Chicano novel of all time. Maybe I'll teach it." I knew if I said, "Nobody teaches it," the takeaway would be, "you need to teach it" or "he's calling us out." So I said, "Maybe I'll teach it." Sure enough, the ninth grade team said, "No, we want it. We're going to do it next year." They've been doing it for the last 2 years.

Managing Anxiety

A deep dive produces anxiety, and the deeper the dive, the greater the anxiety—for both the leader and the organization. Part of the work of "diving" into any dilemma is uncovering hidden assumptions, organizational norms, and patterns of the past that are in operation, and sensing that business as usual is not serving students and teachers well. Few educators are comfortable when the spotlight turns to their practice and uncovers the ways in which that practice is not meeting students' needs. Moreover, anxiety emerges as members of the community reach their own limits, in terms of identity and constructive developmental frames of reference. A leader or teacher who views the world through a socializing frame might genuinely have trouble stepping back from a dilemma and answering the question "What do *I* really think is best for students?" as separate from district mandates and past school practices.

In Jed's case, his move to head of school began a series of events that uncovered the lack of coherence in teaching philosophy and practices pre-K–12. That slow discovery process, as part of the deep dive, produced considerable anxiety across the school community. Perhaps it caused the most anxiety for Jed himself. The deep dive challenges the identity individuals hold; the deeper the dive, the more identity is challenged. Letting go of a familiar identity and envisioning a new identity is uncomfortable, and to be done successfully likely requires a developmental shift.

As the head of school, when Jed began to ask reflective questions about cross-grade alignment, show teachers data that suggested discrepancies, and connect this data to student achievement over time, both he and the organization became unsettled. Without consistent supports, this observing and uncovering process can become too unsettling, too quickly. Leaders must anticipate organizational anxiety and not let it rattle them. Leaders, alone and with colleagues, have to simultaneously uncover patterns of the past and build enough capacity for the whole organization to make sense of and address large, systemic issues. Ignoring, avoiding, or minimizing anxiety won't necessarily help.

Similarly, Liz describes the anxiety that was raised when she and the school's teachers started changing what it looked like and sounded like to learn in school:

> One of the biggest anxieties—this probably moves toward dread—is when you do something different and you're breaking traditions. Even traditions like desks in rows, lectures, and worksheets, because you are trying to do more interdisciplinary, inquiry-oriented learning. And then saying "and they will do fine on the state test"— that has still been hard. I've experienced it, I've had great luck with it, but it still feels like you're walking out on air when you say "We're not going to do test prep—we're going to do great teaching."

Liz had to remind teachers, students, families, the broader community, and herself that students were gaining critical experiences, skills, and learning.

In what Heifetz et al. (2009) describe as adaptive leadership work, they suggest that in order to solve large, adaptive challenges, leaders must create a "holding environment" (p. 154) and "regulate the heat" (p. 158) to ensure that anxiety levels are not rising too fast. In creating a holding environment (another facet of constructive developmental theory), leaders create conversational or situational opportunities that "provide safety and structure for people to surface and discuss the particular values, perspectives, and creative ideas they have on the challenging situation they all face" (p. 155).

This will look different across schools and districts, but often entails setting norms, using agendas and structures to guide discussions, and creating mechanisms for tabling ideas and returning to them later when conversations get too heated. Heifetz et al. also advise leaders to "lower the 'heat' in [community members'] organizational lives" (p. 158) so that anxiety levels do not rise to the point where faculty and staff are paralyzed or angered to the point of disengagement. This makes good sense, and sounds simple enough, but managing organizational anxiety throughout the deep dive is one of the most critical (and often overlooked) elements of the work.

CULTURE, CAPACITY, AND ANXIETY:
IT ALL WORKS TOGETHER

In Jed and Liz's stories, starting the deep dive involved attending to culture, capacity, and anxiety. Culture was being uncovered, capacity was being built, and anxiety was being both raised and managed. Embedded in the stories were the principles of slowing down, sharing practice, and embracing discomfort. Now, as we move to Chapter 4, we explore some of the concrete strategies and processes associated with this first phase of the deep dive.

Observing

In Practice

People hired you because of things you did at the last place—and presumably you were good at it, or it went well—and so they want you to do the same thing or something similar in this place. But what if it's not what this place needs? I need to learn what this place needs, and about this place, and who it is, and what it is trying to do.

—Liz Ozuna

When Liz Ozuna began as the founding principal of the Mathis High School for International Studies, she knew that she had to start by learning about what the school needed. Alongside this new learning, Liz had to let go of what had worked well at her previous school. She needed to learn more about the Mathis students, teachers, and community. She needed to focus on "what *this* place needed" before initiating any kind of a dive. Moreover, Liz knew that she couldn't do this learning alone. She needed to engage the faculty and staff to join her to discover who they are, as teachers and adult learners, as they opened this new school together. She needed the observing phase of the deep dive.

Liz and the faculty were developing a new high school with an emphasis on global learning, which would be located on the campus of an existing high school (the only high school in this rural south Texas town). As a first step, in the summer months before the school opened in August and then into the school year, Liz and the Mathis school community began learning together as a community of adult learners. They read together, asked questions of each other as well as of students and families, looked at teacher and student work, observed in classrooms in their school, and visited other schools. Liz and the Mathis faculty began this deep dive by observing and uncovering—and helping others to observe and uncover—patterns of the past. These were not only patterns at the existing high school in Mathis but also long-standing expectations about how high schools work. She was preparing herself and the group to let go of patterns that might not serve their students or school well in the future.

TOOLS FOR OBSERVING AND UNCOVERING

As we described in previous chapters, starting a deep dive requires observing cultural patterns and practices and then letting them go in order to build a new and better future. "Observing" requires helping adults become more complex thinkers about their practice while simultaneously managing the organizational anxiety that inevitably surfaces. This chapter continues to explore these ideas, in practice, by answering the question, "What does it look like to begin the observing phase of the deep dive, to simultaneously uncover patterns of the past, support adult development, and manage anxiety?"

When Schools Are Trapped in Patterns of the Past

Imagine the following scenario of a faculty meeting—and if you have worked in a school for any length of time, we are betting that this scenario will seem all too familiar.

A group of new teachers enters the auditorium and finds their place somewhere near the middle, avoiding the front row but also steering clear of the teachers sitting at the very back, with empty rows of seats separating them from the rest of the group. People straggle in after the start of the meeting and dart into seats. A few teachers openly grade papers, while others surreptitiously check email, chitchat, or doodle on the agenda.

The principal stands at the front and runs down a list of announcements, usually including upcoming procedures for the next round of tests being administered, the latest update on safety drills, parent meetings and progress reports, and student events teachers are asked to attend. Teachers become annoyed at questions that seem to extend the length of the meeting. New teachers don't dare to ask questions. The principal seems as eager to leave as the teachers.

This not-so-fictional scene of a faculty meeting displays all of the characteristics of isolationism, conservatism, and presentism (Hargreaves & Shirley, 2009; Lortie, 1975) that prevent deep change in schools. These patterns prevent teachers and leaders from even seeing the hidden norms that exist in schools. Protocols are tools that can upend these typical faculty meetings and business as usual, to help us see and disrupt patterns that keep us mired in the past. In the following sections, we illustrate how protocols can be used in the dive's first phase.

Protocols Support Observing

Protocols are one of the primary tools Jed, Liz, and the other leaders we interviewed used to effectively navigate the first phase of their respective deep dives. These leaders, collectively, employed protocols to:

1. Support the cultural observation and meaning-making necessary to uncover, examine, and modify hidden norms and values
2. Intentionally encourage adult development
3. Manage the inevitable organizational anxiety that arises when culture is initially examined

In this chapter, in order to provide readers with a handful of tools that might support the observation phase of a deep dive, we zoom in on protocols and related professional practices. While there are dozens of tools and strategies available, we describe just a handful that we have found to be representative and most useful in this phase.

What Are Protocols?

As noted in the previous chapter, Jed Lippard, when head of school of Prospect Hill Academy, intentionally adopted the mindset of "chief adult developer" to build the capacity of the entire school community. Moreover, he is quick to suggest that the use of protocols was one of his key strategies for supporting such developmental work. Jed states: "I would say that, from my own leadership, there are two things that I don't know if I could function without. One is some knowledge about developmental theory. . . . Two is actually the use of protocols." Similarly, we found protocols to be essential tools for the leaders we interviewed, particularly at the outset of a deep dive.

Protocols may be defined as structures for having conversations, facilitating collaboration, and helping educators learn new ways of working together (McDonald, Mohr, Dichter, & McDonald, 2013). They are scaffolded conversations that follow designated steps, often with identified time limits. Like teaching strategies for student learning, protocols are strategies for supporting and encouraging adult learning and development. They should be enacted with fidelity, especially initially, as these steps work together to help participants have conversations that are unfamiliar and can feel risky. Adhering to the processes and time frames of a protocol builds familiarity and makes associated risk more manageable. Common objectives of protocols include enlarging understanding, revealing assumptions, identifying new possibilities, and/or naming tensions.

The Consultancy Protocol: An Example

One of the most useful and frequently used protocols is the Consultancy Protocol (Dunne, Evans, & Thompson-Grove, 2018). In order to understand how protocols work, it might be helpful to analyze the steps of this foundational structured conversation:

Consultancy Protocol

1. Presentation of the dilemma
2. Clarifying questions
3. Probing questions
4. Discussion of the dilemma
5. Presenter's reflection on the conversation
6. Debriefing of the process (Dunne, Evans, & Thompson-Grove 2018)

A preliminary step in the protocol is for a presenter to identify a dilemma, a "puzzle . . . that raises questions, an idea that seems to have conceptual gaps, or something about process or product that you just can't figure out" (Dunne, Evan, & Thompson-Grove, 2018, p. 1). Even this first identification requires a good deal of observing current practices and noticing potential gaps between espoused values and ensuing actions.

Once a dilemma has been identified, the presenter meets with a facilitator in a preconference to plan for the discussion and identify a focus/framing question, artifacts that may be required for better understanding of the dilemma, and where anxiety might be present in the examination of the dilemma so that the facilitator can anticipate (not avoid) it.

Together, the facilitator and presenter bring that dilemma to a small group of colleagues for consideration and discussion (Step 1). The facilitator supports the presenter by leading the group through a series of deliberate conversational moves. This series of events both supports and teaches a group how to slow down thinking and observe, clarify, and understand before leaping to a solution.

Participants are asked to listen during the presentation, not interrupt, and not provide immediate recommendations. Then come the questions. Starting with clarifying questions (Step 2) allows the group to better understand the presenter's context. Probing questions (Step 3) support the entire group (and particularly the presenter) in expanding and deepening thinking, uncovering hidden assumptions and beliefs, and prompting different ways of viewing the same set of facts.

The discussion of the dilemma (Step 4) is not a rush to solve the dilemma. In this step, participants share what they heard, identify assumptions, surface salient features of the dilemma, and consider new, shared understandings. This goes against the grain of business as usual in schools, where educators all too often leap to solutions in 3-minute hallway conversations. The presenter listens during this step and is not involved in the discussion. The presenter then has time to offer reflections (Step 5) on what stood out or seemed meaningful, naming next steps the group might take. Remember, the dilemma is owned by the presenter, who is given "the last word" on the dilemma itself. Finally, as with all protocol-based discussions, the facilitator ends by asking the group to debrief the process (Step 6). This final step helps the group improve over time by determining whether and how well the protocol served the presenter's needs, how the group worked together, and how the facilitation served the presenter, the dilemma, and the group.

While not all protocols share these exact same steps, our description reflects many of the mindsets embedded in all protocols:

- Seeking to clarify and observe first, before solving
- Seeking to understand and create shared meaning through questioning
- Allowing the presenter to own the dilemma and its solution by not immediately offering a list of possible actions.

Underlying Principles of Protocols

It is important that leaders understand the principles upon which protocols such as the Consultancy are built, principles that support the observing phase of a deep dive. Protocols support three "'against the grain' interactions . . . : (1) slowing down, (2) sharing practice, and (3) embracing discomfort" (Breidenstein et al., 2012, p. 85). They are "against the grain" because they push against the conservatism, isolationism, and presentism that characterize many schools (Hargreaves & Shirley, 2009; Lortie, 1975).

"Slowing down" means describing before judging, asking questions before recommending, and making room for many voices and perspectives. "Sharing practice" includes not only an educator putting work or dilemmas on the table for others to see, but also group members contributing experiences, insights, and questions. These acts of sharing acknowledge that all participants have wisdom to give. "Embracing discomfort" comes in acknowledging that everyone's work is in progress; everyone has something to learn; everyone has dilemmas; and there are no easy answers to complex questions and issues, especially when tackling inequity.

PROTOCOLS IN ACTION: A TRAJECTORY OF RISK

When using protocols to observe, understand, and shift school culture, it is important to consider how protocols are introduced and sequenced over time. Protocols used early in the observing phase help teachers comfortably share experiences and learn with and from one another without too much risk. Next, different structures can be used to enter into riskier ventures, including examining and exploring adult and student work. More challenging protocols can be used to support educators as they take the risk of observing each other's teaching practice and providing feedback. Finally, another set of protocols can help explore larger dilemmas, hidden assumptions, and even issues of structural inequity and social justice (the riskiest work). We summarize such a trajectory in Table 4.1 (note that all the protocols listed may be found on the website schoolreforminitiative.org).

Liz and Jed used a variety of protocols to help themselves and their organizations observe and understand culture, attend to adult development, and manage anxiety. In the following sections, using the progression depicted in Table 4.1, we present these protocols and related stories in order of increasing risk. Collectively, the stories focus on community development: looking at text, adult work, student work, data, and teaching practice through shared observation. Ultimately, Liz and Jed sought to provide teachers the opportunity to see, hear, and inquire into individual and collective practices. They were helping their schools uncover, discover, and begin to deconstruct visible artifacts and practices as they began various deep dives.

Observing and Understanding Community

In Mathis, Liz was starting a new school, which meant that she was building a culture while helping the faculty examine the beliefs and assumptions that they were bringing.

First Protocols. Liz began with check-ins and community-building activities and protocols such as Connections (Thompson-Grove, 2018a) and Compass Points (School Reform Initiative, 2018c) that helped the staff explore who they were as individuals and as a group. This was when the group was first coming together in the planning summer months and start of the school year.

Liz used The World Café (2018) process to build community and start initial conversations in August, first with teachers to learn together and to build familiarity with the process, and then with students and families:

Family World Café Questions:

- What hopes do you have for your students at this new school?
- What concerns do you have for your students at this new school?
- What should parental support and involvement look like in this new school?

Table 4.1 Protocols Useful in Observing, Understanding, and Shifting Culture

Trajectory of Risk	Protocol Category	Examples of Protocols
Less intensity, degree of trust required, and amount of time the group has been meeting	Observing and understanding community	Compass Points, Connections, Chalk Talk, Continuum Dialogue, Block Party, Microlab, Passion Profiles
	Discussing text	Three Levels of Text, Text-Rendering, Chalk Talk, Final Word, Four "A"s, Save the Last Word for Me, Microlab, Text-Based Seminar, Block Party
	Looking at student work	Collaborative Assessment Conference, ATLAS: Learning from Student Work, Student Work Gallery, The Slice
	Looking at and tuning adult work	Tuning Protocol, Tuning a Plan, Constructivist Tuning Protocol, Tuning for Larger Groups
	Looking at data	ATLAS: Looking at Data, Data Driven Dialogue, Data Mining Protocol, The Slice
	Planning and observing	Into-/Through-/Beyond- Planning Guide, Lesson-Planning/Observation Guide, Video Camera, Court Reporter, Focus Point, Interesting Moments, Observer as Learner, Person Observed as Coach
	Dilemmas of practice	Consultancy, Issaquah, Charrette, Back to the Future Protocol
Increasing intensity, degree of trust required, and amount of time the group has been meeting	Equity and social justice	Equity Protocol, Equity Stances, Looking at Student Work: Equity, Classroom Equity Writing Prompt, Provocative Prompts for Equity Conversations, Tuning for Equity Protocol

Note. Adapted from "Professional Learning as the Key to Linking Content and Literacy Instruction," by J. Ippolito, in J. Ippolito, J. F. Lawrence, & C. Zaller (Eds.), *Adolescent Literacy in the Era of the Common Core: From Research into Practice* (pp. 215–234), 2013, Cambridge, MA: Harvard Education Press.

Student and Educator World Café Questions:

- What does our school look like?
- How do student learn?
- How do teachers teach?
- What hopes do you have for yourself at this new school?
- What personal gifts do you bring to this new school?

Liz's questions regarding hopes for the new school were similar across different audiences (teachers, students, and families) but were also personalized for each group. This experience helped Liz, teachers, students and families to listen, uncover assumptions, and build community.

Looking at Text. In the fall of their first year together as a faculty and as a school, Liz introduced text-based protocols in monthly faculty meetings. Her goals were to build capacity for more difficult conversations, practice using and facilitating protocols, and perhaps try out the discomfort that can come with sharing an opinion that differs from a colleague's or reading a text you disagree with (a reflective activity that also builds adult-development capacities). Discussing text can feel less risky than discussing each other's work, so it can be a place to build collaborative practice. The faculty engaged in a book-study of Ted and Nancy Sizer's *The Students Are Watching* (1999) using a variety of text-based protocols, for example, the Text-Rendering protocol (School Reform Initiative, 2018d). Faculty participants identified a significant sentence, phrase, and word in Chapter 2 of the Sizers' book. These responses were charted and read aloud as the newly "rendered" text, followed by a discussion. Liz's discussion questions included:

- What comments can you share about the reading overall?
- What connections can you see between your experience reading this text and what the Sizers say about "grappling"?
- How will this text-rendering experience (process), and the information you gleaned from the chapter (content), translate back to your classroom?

After the discussion, Liz used reflective writing to capture new thinking and emerging learning. She invited faculty to provide feedback throughout the book study and protocol discussions to express concerns and uncover anxiety.

Text-based protocols focus on slowing down the conversation, exploring different perspectives, and building a shared understanding of an important idea rather than coming to "the right answer." While many text-based discussions in schools focus on adult learning—for example, how to teach a new reading strategy or what the new English language learner standards require—protocols can provide countercultural, developmental experiences with elements of challenge, rigor, and support.

Protocols for Looking at Adult Work

Liz continued diving deeper, from community-building activities and text-based protocols to looking together at adult work. She modeled by first asking groups of teachers to look at her own principal work and then the school's shared work. Leaders we interviewed knew that if the observing phase was going to be successful, they needed to share their leadership practice as well as ask for feedback before asking others to share their practice.

Tuning Adult Work. In her first months on the job, Liz designed a whole-faculty Tuning protocol (McDonald & Allen, 2017) with a draft vision statement that they had been developing together for the school. With an experienced consultant facilitating, the Tuning protocol began with Liz presenting a draft of the vision statement she had developed from teachers' initial input. After Liz presented the draft, the group asked clarifying questions and, after some time to pause and consider where the vision statement met the mark and fell short of the mark, they provided first "warm" and then "cool" feedback while Liz listened and took notes. The process concluded with an opportunity for Liz to reflect out loud on the feedback and her next steps, and then the group debriefed the process. Liz made sure her work was among the first the group looked at so she could model the process and be the first to risk receiving warm and cool feedback publicly.

Looking Together at Data. Schools often look at data as a way to think more deeply about student and adult work (McDonald et al., 2018). At Prospect Hill Academy, Jed and the leadership team codeveloped data-analysis processes that slowed down the conversation by including more description. While digging into the data was important, the Prospect Hill team also wanted to surface and learn from the teaching practices underlying the data. Throughout the process, they knew they needed to address initial discomfort, particularly around looking at student-learning outcomes. Jed shared, "We invented [our own] Data Wise system at our school, which is to look at data broadly defined, to assess how the data speaks to the objectives" (see Data Wise website at datawise.gse.harvard.edu). Three questions guided the analysis:

- Which objectives did we meet?
- Which objectives did we not meet?
- What needs improvement?

Their process was deliberately designed to build capacity to effectively observe and learn from their shared data and practices. The conversations not only focused on looking at the data, but equally important were implications for instructional interventions. Jed talked openly about using data-analysis conversations to start talking about current practices. He wanted to surface teachers' assumptions as well as the possibility of new, shared practices.

In many schools the conversation stops after the data analysis. Teachers go back to their individual rooms to work in silos without ongoing collaboration to explore implications for individual and collective action. McDonald and his colleagues (2018) offer smart, thoughtful, and practical "new directions" recommendations for data analysis and use, including a focus on building teacher community; they also provide well-researched school profiles of data-analysis work in action. Together Jed, the leadership team, and teachers at Prospect Hill Academy executed interventions they developed together as a result of looking at data. Then, as Jed encouraged, they would "dipstick again" and repeat the process, diving deeper each time.

Protocols for Looking at Student Work

Early in his work as a leader at Prospect Hill, Jed knew that he wanted to change the most visible artifacts of student learning—tests—and the pattern of direct instruction and traditional assessment underlying that system: "I had to undo that in a big way. We need to get our kids in front of people they don't know on a regular basis to defend and explain their work." Jed saw the predominant pattern of the past—paper-and-pencil tests—as impeding more creative and deep thinking by students. Thus he asked teachers to look together at student work and to collaboratively develop learning experiences with rigorous, creative, and authentic artifacts of learning that could be displayed in student work exhibitions. Protocols such as the ATLAS: Learning from Student Work (School Reform Initiative, 2018a), Student Work Gallery (Thompson-Grove, 2018c), and Collaborative Assessment Conference (School Reform Initiative, 2018b) were key tools in helping the faculty make sense of student work and design more authentic demonstrations of student learning.

Protocols for Observing Adult Practice

At Mathis, Liz understood that trust had to be scaffolded. She supported her community as they slowly worked toward riskier peer observation. She believed such observations would be an important step in shaping a more collaborative culture and building capacity for challenging work. Liz decided to begin by observing students' portfolio presentations in a peer network school. Observing in a partner school built observational skills and provided new insights about teaching and learning.

Liz framed the observation around four questions:

- What are students asked to do?
- How does this presentation seem to connect to a bigger picture?
- What questions, concerns, or comments does this raise for you?
- What implications do you see for our work at Mathis High School for International Studies?

As the teachers shared their observations in a structured debrief, the group uncovered assumptions and questions about assessment, student portfolios, and what the 4-year experience of students should be in high school. Teachers were grappling with an assessment system other than a traditional one with homework, quizzes, and tests.

A significant deepening of observing occurred when Liz designed an observing experience involving Mathis families. She had been hearing directly and through the grapevine that parents were concerned about "noisy classrooms." Parents seemed to associate this with a lack of discipline, while Liz and the faculty thought noise was a result of active pedagogy being enacted in the new school. So mid-spring of the first year, Liz took a risk by inviting families to observe classrooms, knowing this would both uncover and disturb school culture and build new, shared understanding. She structured a School Walk observation (Fraser, 2017) with a framing question. Teachers were hesitant about classroom observations; this was definitely not business as usual, and anxiety was high. Liz fostered open dialogue and worked with faculty to determine what would minimize that anxiety.

The day of the observations Liz gave family participants a focusing question about noise levels, clipboards, and an hour to observe. "You have full access to the school. Look around. See if it is as noisy as you assume, and see if you understand why." Parents shared their observations, which Liz charted. "Frankly, they pointed out some things to me that I hadn't seen. I got some real honest feedback, and a couple of those people became some of my most involved parents."

Liz then engaged the faculty in an analysis of that same data using the Collaborative Assessment Conference protocol (School Reform Initiative, 2018b). They discovered that some of the concern could be traced to the actual building itself, which did not have sound insulation. They also received feedback on what parents perceived of the classroom instruction: "They didn't think the instruction was bad. In most classrooms they didn't see misbehavior; instead, they saw kids learning and talking. They saw kids learning—and it was really noisy." These conversations built the community's capacity to observe and wrestle with patterns of the past (i.e., rows of desks and silent classrooms) and make room for new, innovative, and potentially less comfortable practices (i.e., "noisy" constructivist classrooms). Liz explains, "We were challenging fundamental notions about what a classroom looks like."

The protocols, and Liz's deliberate use of them in sequence, slowed down the observation and uncovering process. The structures and the sequence Liz utilized encouraged considered reactions and guarded against jumping to conclusions. And they addressed the teachers' and families' anxiety head-on by acknowledging the anxiety and using transparent structures and clear processes with known objectives. The community was learning to observe.

SUPPORTING OBSERVING WITH PROTOCOLS

In summary, protocols support the observing phase of a deep dive in three ways: (1) understanding culture, (2) promoting adult development, and (3) managing anxiety. Uncovering cultural patterns, supporting adults in becoming more complex thinkers, and managing the inevitable ensuing anxiety are important for letting go in order to begin the turn to a better future and better practice.

Protocols Support Understanding School Culture

Sustained change begins with observing and understanding culture. Protocols and routines encourage a group to step back from and name their own experiences, better see everyday occurrences as the product of particular cultural norms, and make sense of collectively held beliefs, assumptions, and practices. Protocols build shared language and structures that support slower, deeper thinking. This foundational work allows leaders and faculty to stave off the rush to action associated with the Common Theory.

Protocols Promote Adult Development

Protocols promote adult development in three ways: (1) They construct a "holding environment" (Drago-Severson, 2009; Kegan, 1998) with support and challenge; (2) they provide opportunities for groups to surface, share, and shape norms; and (3) they prompt reflective thinking and increasingly complex questioning that lead to deeper, shared understandings about complex issues.

First, a good "holding environment" supports an individual's current frame, challenges that existing frame to consider "more complex ways of knowing," and provides "continuity, stability, and availability" for individual or group development (Drago-Severson, 2009, pp. 56–57). Protocols create holding environments that allow educators to come into conversations at different places in their thinking and practice and collectively grow into new ways of seeing, thinking, and understanding their work.

Second, protocols offer opportunities for groups to surface, share, and shape norms and agreements for engaging in difficult conversations and challenging work. Each protocol offers steps and modes of participation that can be quite different from day-to-day meetings and conversations. Protocols provide a sense of structure and predictability, which help stabilize the group as it slowly builds capacity to tackle larger and larger dilemmas.

Third, protocols help groups learn to ask and "sit with" more nuanced and challenging questions. Groups learn the difference between concrete clarifying questions and deeper or more abstract questions that uncover assumptions, dilemmas, and paradoxes. Over time, individuals and groups differentiate among and deploy these different types of questions, building capacity for reflection and collaboration.

Protocols Support Managing Anxiety

Observing and naming existing cultural norms is almost always uncomfortable and creates anxiety. It surfaces deeply held assumptions that raise questions of identity. "Am I a good teacher?" or "What is good work?" are examples of questions about identity that regularly surface as schools learn to observe. Not only do identity issues arise, but because a deep dive is begun without full knowledge of where the dive will lead, unavoidable and considerable anxiety is generated.

Protocols and holding environments can surface the "elephants in the room" (Heifetz et al., 2009, p. 102) or what Barth (2006) might term "nondiscussables." These are "subjects sufficiently important that they are talked about frequently but are so laden with anxiety and fearfulness that these conversations take place only in the parking lot, the restrooms, the playground, the carpool, or the dinner table at home" (p. 8). Protocols help bring "the elephants into the room" and the "nondiscussables" back into the faculty, team, or department meeting.

Protocols also help manage anxiety by creating language for discussing and observing aspects of school life (teacher work, student work, dilemmas of practice, and so on) that might otherwise always remain "nondiscussable." Protocols do this by delaying or eliminating judgment. Rounds of discussion focus on "noticing," "clarifying," or "probing"—all before participants are allowed to offer suggestions for next steps. Protocols end with reflection and debriefing. They have places where the "heat" (anxiety) may be raised but also where it is lowered (Heifetz et al., 2009, pp. 29–30). This conversation is very different from business as usual, when educators often offer unsolicited (and sometimes unkind) advice to one another in schools without first seeking to truly understand the dilemma at hand. If adult development is the aim, then anxiety is anticipated and accepted as part of that process. That includes the leader's own anxiety as well as others' anxiety.

PREPARING FOR THE TURN: THE SECOND PHASE OF THE DEEP DIVE

As mentioned in Chapter 1, the Common Theory is characterized by a sprint from problem identification, to implementation, to assessment; however, there is little evidence to suggest that such a leap to action produces the long-lasting and deep changes that schools today desperately need (McDonald, 2014). Instead, we suggest that the deep dive into school reinvention must begin with a phase of observing and uncovering of hidden norms. In Chapters 3 and 4, we argued that the capacity for the leader to change their school is rooted in uncovering culture, building collective capacity with attention to adult development, and accepting that raised anxiety can be both a positive and a challenging force.

As leaders continue to dive deeper into the harbor of school reinvention, they must wrestle with their own capacity for going public with a major school reinvention effort; they must assess whether the timing is right to instigate deep reinvention; and they must consider how to harness the power of others within the organization. We address all of these ideas and more in the next two chapters (Chapters 5 and 6), which describe the phase we call "turning."

CHAPTER 5

Turning
The Second Phase of the Deep Dive

What will happen when class and race rears its ugly head, as it inevitably will? How will our understanding and commitment to the long-term benefit of creating a socially and economically diverse school be challenged?

—Matt Underwood

At the Atlanta Neighborhood Charter School (ANCS) in Atlanta, Georgia, Executive Director Matt Underwood shared, "I was personally nagged by the persistent loss over the past few years of racial and economic diversity among our student population." There was a growing gap between the first tenet of the school's mission to "build an empowered and inclusive community of students, parents, and educators," and diminishing student diversity. Matt knew that "everyone would agree that explicitly taking on this gap is important." However, he also suspected that many members of the school community held only a surface understanding of the issue and would soon discover that the intentional reframing of their practices would challenge every aspect of the school. He wondered,

> How will our understanding and commitment to the long-term benefit of creating a socially and economically diverse school be challenged? What will it mean for faculty members to intentionally examine and reshape their teaching practices to meet the needs of a more highly diverse classroom? What will happen when supportive community members realize that a change in admission practices results in their own students not being admitted?

In his 9 years at ANCS Matt used many of the strategies of the observing movement of the deep dive. Matt engaged the entire community in a sustained planning process around the mission of the school, helped the faculty examine demographic data and student work, organized a State of the School meeting, wrote a blog that focused on issues of equity at ANCS, and used texts about race, class, and equitable educational practice to frame faculty and community meetings. Matt intentionally led a deep dive into the school's assumptions about diversity and equity and along the way built the school's capacity for looking into its practice, exposing, exploring, and even rethinking fundamental assumptions, and staying in uncomfortable conversations.

Matt and the school sensed a new, more equitable future was possible, but they still needed to make the "turn" toward this new future. Without the turn, the school might exist in a perpetual cycle of talking about, evaluating, and brainstorming, but never enacting, a new future. Turning requires not only clearly seeing the organization as it is, but also enacting a yet-unknown and risky future.

THE TURN AT ATLANTA NEIGHBORHOOD CHARTER SCHOOL

Matt describes his approach to the turn simply. "I don't know if I can pinpoint what the start was. It had been nagging at me personally for a few years, the dwindling economic diversity of the school. It's one of those things that nobody's telling you that you need to do something about." Matt's explanation makes two key points about the turn. First, it is personal. In the deepest of deep dives, the turn affects everyone—faculty, parents, administrators, students, and board members—individually and collectively. At ANCS, for example, starting the turn toward enacting a new future asks what it means to be a teacher whose practice is grounded in educational equity. For parents, entering the turn asks about the difference a weighted admissions policy might make for their child's classroom or even attendance at the school. For Matt and the principals of the elementary and middle schools, the turn asks them to interrogate their personnel, budgetary, and administrative practices *and* to manage their own anxiety and the anxiety of the entire community.

Besides being personal, the turn, Matt suggests, is not something that you *have* to do. "Nobody's telling you that you need to do something." In fact, many schools comfortably, and perhaps even sensibly, avoid the anxiety, risk, and worry that making the turn entails. Matt describes how at ANCS, the focus on equity and diversity "wasn't just coming from me. This was really a part of the fabric of the school from the beginning and a unique and important feature of who we are as a community." Yet, despite this seemingly fundamental commitment, "the school, for a number of different reasons, was more socioeconomically diverse in those early years than it is now."

In Schein's (2016) terms, the "espoused values" of the school were about equity, but somehow at the deeper level, the school had drifted away from its espoused values. Matt notes, "Equity is something that, on the surface, everybody can agree to, and then you get into it, and it is more challenging than you might first imagine." Matt cannot resolve these issues by introducing a new reading initiative, acquiring new textbooks, or even requiring mandatory diversity trainings for faculty. He has to first observe and understand the organization, help others to do the same, and then slowly turn the school toward enacting a new, more complicated, and possibly more dangerous future.

THE TURN AT NORTH READING MIDDLE SCHOOL

Cathy O'Connell from North Reading Middle School in North Reading, Massachusetts, confirms Matt's observations. Leading a multiyear deep dive called North Reading Middle School 2.0 (NRMS 2.0), Cathy and the assistant principal Michael Maloney helped the school "see" its own structures and practices as well as discover other possibilities. Cathy, like Matt, spent time helping the faculty look at data and best practices, building leadership capacity, holding parent meetings, using protocols to look at student and teacher work, writing to the community, and engaging the superintendent. She created an NRMS 2.0 Leadership Team made up of teachers from every grade level and content area, as well as a group of parents. For over a year, Cathy supported the school community as it looked deeply at its own unexamined practices and explored new possibilities. The charge of NRMS 2.0 was to examine every aspect of the school—student grouping, curriculum, instruction, adult collaboration, community partnerships, and relationships between faculty and students. However, as was the case with Matt Underwood, Cathy's thorniest and deepest issue was around equity.

At North Reading Middle School there was a tradition of leveling kids by ability starting in 6th grade. As with Matt, Cathy's issue was personal. She says, "I was a parent here, and an assistant principal in a different system, and was shocked when my son came home at the end of 6th grade with a letter that outlined his levels." She continued, "When I say that it's not equitable, it's inequitable for the kid, when they come home with this letter that tells them, 'This is what teachers think of me'; it's a self-fulfilling prophecy. They think, 'I'm a Level Two, and then I'm going to be a Level Two.'" Cathy cared deeply about this issue, not just because of her commitment to a certain math program or approach to science, but because of who she is. The deepest deep dives are personal.

Cathy also made the choice to dive deeply into issues of equity and eventually to turn toward a new future at her school when she became the principal. Like Matt, no one told her she had to. She had no directive from the school board or superintendent. She just knew: "It's not equitable. At the very core, in my belly it's not equitable. Students weren't given an equal opportunity to learn at a high level. They weren't given an equal opportunity for high-level instruction. They were given a substandard or subpar opportunity." Both Matt and Cathy understand that the deepest dives, which often are about fundamental issues of equity, define and clarify their own identity and the identity of schools they lead.

Cathy knew when it was time to let go of past practices and enact a new future. Observing, seeing, understanding, and considering new possibilities was essential work, but it did not enact a new future for the school or its students. "I think I felt it was time to put something down in writing. That's when I felt I needed to take control and put it out there. Whether it was totally changed after we talked about it as a group, I was okay with that, but I thought it was time."

After a year of visiting other schools, working with parents, holding faculty meetings, and leading the NRMS 2.0 effort, after a year of seeing and understanding the downloaded patterns of the past, Cathy understood that she—and the school—had to turn to and embrace their future. "Yeah, we really needed movement. We needed to see our work come to fruition. I think also we were probably afraid, but at some point you've got to grab hold and say, 'This is what we're going to do.'" After the turn, Cathy noted, "Our general questions, our bigger question had gone from *what* to *how*." NRMS turned from observing and understanding itself to enacting its future.

SCHOOL CULTURE

Both Matt and Cathy know that reframing their personal and school practices will affect every aspect of the school and its community—from admissions to teaching and learning, grouping for instruction, personnel decisions, and relationships among students, teachers, and the community. Cathy noted, "When you change something like leveling in a school that's always leveled, that's a deep dive into fundamental stuff with the school. It doesn't get too much more fundamental than that." The reason is that the deeper the dive, the more it disturbs the hidden and powerful fundamental assumption of a school's culture.

Drawing on Schein (2016), we earlier conceptualized the relationship between the deep dive and organizational culture as shown in Figure 5.1.

In this conceptualization, much of what passes for school reform or improvement—what we call the Common Theory—takes place at the level of visible artifacts (schedules, dress codes, building layout, programs, initiatives, and so on). Visible artifacts are easy to discern but hard to understand because they rest upon invisible—and powerful—assumptions. They are also often the focus of the Common Theory. A deeper dive involves espoused values. *Espoused values* are the articulated strategies, goals,

Figure 5.1. Shallow and Deep Dives

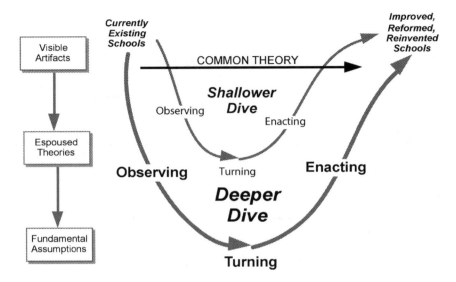

and philosophies communicated by an organization. School vision and mission statements, strategic plans, or guiding principles are examples of espoused values. They reflect "what we say we do." It is not unusual for a school or district to spend productive time on mission statements or other espoused values.

However, the deepest dives touch fundamental and often hidden assumptions. If espoused values are "what we say we do," then fundamental assumptions are "what we actually believe and do." Substantive reform, and especially the reinvention of schools, lies in seeing the tensions between espoused values and fundamental assumptions and diving into longstanding competing commitments and unarticulated traditions.

The Power of Culture

Both Matt Underwood and Cathy O'Connell acknowledge that fundamental assumptions are powerful levers for change that are difficult to see and master. Cathy noted, "Our leveling permeates everything that happens in this building. From the technical stuff to the adaptive stuff, it permeates everything." Matt described how easy it is to avoid facing a school's fundamental assumptions. "You have all these challenges, and dealing with something that has to do with class and with race quickly falls down people's priority list." So why is disturbing a school's culture such difficult work?

As we introduced in Chapter 2, Schein (2016) defines organizational culture as

> a pattern of shared, basic assumptions that the group learned as it solved its problems of external adaptation and internal integration, that has worked well enough to be considered valid and, therefore, to be taught to new members as the correct way to perceive, think, and feel in relation to those problems. (p. 12)

Much of the power of organizational cultures derives from the fact that they are (1) shared, (2) learned, and (3) at some point in time worked well. It is useful to consider each of these characteristics identified by Schein.

First, organizational culture is a "pattern of shared . . . assumptions." These assumptions are hidden and never put in the teacher handbook or collective bargaining agreement. Questions such as whose voice is valued and whose is not, how space and time are managed, what "good teaching" is, or what students are capable of are questions answered by the culture of a school. For example, at NRMS, the deep value of grouping by ability was shared by faculty, parents, and students. Cathy describes the power of this shared value: "I don't think I would have had any buy-in, or any support from anyone, if I had just said after my first year, 'We're not doing that anymore, we are eliminating leveling.'" Other common examples of deeply shared assumptions in schools are dividing time into content-specific blocks, the value of seniority among faculty, the division of academic and specialist subjects, and how some students are more "capable" than others. Digging even deeper, schools are also built upon shared assumptions about race, privilege, power, and the purpose of schooling.

Second, organizational culture is made up of "basic assumptions that the group learned." For all its enduring importance and broad influence, organizational culture is learned, and consequently taught by the group to new members. Adjusting, manipulating, or changing the culture of a school—while difficult—is a learning and teaching task. Like any learning, culture cannot be purchased, imposed, ordered, or mandated. The Common Theory has little sway over school culture. A teacher cannot command a 3rd-grader to read at grade level—they have to be taught. Similarly, a leader cannot impose a particular culture in a school; the culture has to be taught and learned, often repeatedly over a period of time. Matt explains this process at ANCS, "We know it's not going to be easy. We know it's probably going to have challenges for different people, but we're committed to it, and we hope they come along with us and help us."

Third, organizational cultures exist because they have "worked well enough to be considered valid." A particular culture exists because at some point it solved a problem for the organization. Although research suggests that many basic assumptions—such as how time is used, how students are grouped for instruction, or the nature of good teaching— need to be reevaluated, educators can be resistant because the established ways of organizing students, academic content, and classroom practice have in fact worked, to some degree, at some time, for many students and teachers.

Culture as Both a Powerful Obstacle and a Support

North Reading Middle School was not a school in crisis and had used an ability-grouping structure for decades. No one could even remember when tracking started, but everyone knew that the school had had good success. The fact that any basic assumptions can be "considered valid" contributes to the fact that educators are often suspicious of change, and that the more a change touches on deep-seated cultural assumptions, the more anxiety the change causes. More than one person at NRMS wondered, "Why are we changing something that works?"

Organizational culture is both a powerful obstacle *and* support for organizational learning and change. Disturbing organizational culture is a risky, anxiety-producing enterprise for both the school and the school leader. Yet any change that does not disturb organizational culture is likely to be superficial and short-lived, just another application of the Common Theory.

If the school does not have the capacity to see, observe, and understand its own downloaded patterns, then it might never make the turn toward enactment. It might just get lost in the weeds of self-study. On the other hand, a school can make the turn too soon, when it is still working at the level of visible artifacts or espoused values. In this case, a school might end up with a new, well-crafted mission statement that looks good at the main entrance but is actually full of unexamined practices, unanswered questions, and business as usual. The question of when to make the turn toward enactment is a critical one for leaders and the schools they lead. Make the turn too soon, and the change is superficial. Wait too long, and the school might never reach enactment. There are several factors that leaders and schools need to consider as they make the turn toward enactment.

WHAT TO EXPECT IN THE TURN

When to enter the turn, and at what depth, is a complex calculation. Not every dive can be the deepest dive into fundamental assumptions; schools also need shallower, more technical dives to carry out the business of school. A dive into a new schedule or mission statement may be needed simply because the school needs a new schedule, tardy policy, or graduation requirement. Moreover, a shallower dive may be all that the school is ready for. A school that has never looked carefully and intentionally at student work or reflected on teaching practice may not have built capacity for the deepest dive into complicated questions of equity similar to the ones led by Cathy O'Connell and Matt Underwood. What factors do schools need to consider when diving deep below the surface of the Common Theory? In our view, there are four, all of which are affected by the depth of the dive.

1. Disturbance of Dominant But Hidden Fundamental Organizational Assumptions

The Common Theory operates at the level of visible artifacts: programs, schedules, codes of conduct, and so on. A deeper dive focuses on espoused values such as mission, values, and guiding principles. The deepest, most difficult dives surface, explore, question, and reframe assumptions about power, identity, and equity. However, the deeper the dive, the more the turn disturbs assumptions of the organization. Schools that have worked only at the level of the Common Theory, that is, with visible artifacts, are most likely not ready for a deep dive into fundamental assumptions. Shallower dives into espoused values such as mission statements or strategic plans might be a productive intermediary.

2. Provocation and Release of Anxiety in the Organization

While the adoption of a different schedule, or a new dress code, can certainly produce anxiety in a school, the deeper a school probes into the difference between its espoused values and what actually happens, the more unsettled, anxious, and apprehensive the school is likely to feel. As a school dives deeply into questions of race, identity, equitable educational practice, what it means to be a teacher, and who students are, the school will most likely become not only anxious but also fearful. As Cathy O'Connell acknowledges, "The deeper we got into issues of leveling and equity, the more complicated and anxious the conversation became." As a dive goes deeper and makes a turn toward enacting a new future, a leader and school can expect anxiety and feelings of instability and worry. Leaders need to consider how much experience the school community has in holding and managing the discomfort that accompanies the deep dive. Schools that have traditionally relied on the Common Theory to minimize anxiety and instability might need to build their capacity for observing, turning, and enacting before engaging in deeper dives.

ANDRES LOPEZ'S STORY 3: TURNING

Andres discovered the complicated and messy work of a deep dive and its fragility.

Now, I'm frustrated with how hard it has been to build on this one Mexican American Literature class. I'm happy that it's growing here, but it needs to be available in a lot more schools. It should be everywhere, all over San Antonio. I'm talking to everyone every time I get a chance. They're probably tired of hearing about it. But right now, it's like a flame that hasn't spread. You can still put it out.

---

3. Opening of the Door to Reinvention

Adopting a new approach to curriculum design or a new literacy strategy can be a useful step in the work of improving schools. Significant research supports the idea that schools where educators continually work together to improve their practice can increase student learning (Bryk, Sebring, Allensworth, Luppescu, & Easton, 2010). However, improving practice is not the same thing as reinventing practice. Improvement builds on what is already assumed to be true, while reinvention questions what has come before, what is assumed to be true. Deep dives into assumptions about who students are; how learning happens; equitable educational practice; the influence of race, class, and gender; or what it means to be a teacher are all deep dives that release expanding amounts of anxiety and simultaneously open the door for reinvention. The deeper the dive, the more the turn disturbs assumptions, provokes anxiety, and opens possibilities for reinvention. Yet most schools have rarely reflected on or shared their practices in ways that allow questioning of foundational assumptions. Thus the deepest dives can be powerful ways of overturning and shifting those assumptions, the very heart of school reinvention.

4. Capacity Required of Both School Leaders and the School

The capacity for a deep dive depends on the ability of the school to resist easy answers, stay in difficult conversations, see value in conflict, consider a variety of perspectives, and persistently ask and live with difficult questions. Using the language of constructive developmental theory (Kegan, 1998) as explained in Chapter 3, schools that undertake the deepest dives need to be less instrumental and more socializing and self-authoring. The deepest dives often require transformative knowing. To make matters more complicated, leaders who lead the deepest dives not only need to lead with "developmental intent" but also may need to be self-authoring or transformative knowers themselves.

Figure 5.2. Four Factors to Consider in the Deep Dive

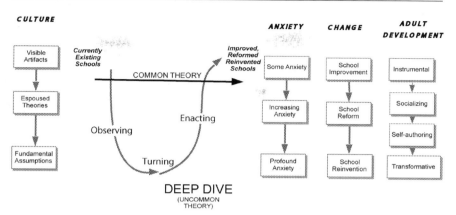

There is no recipe, roadmap, or concrete process—no instrumental path into, through, and out of the deepest dives. The emerging future is always unknown and requires both schools and their leaders to build the capacity to stay in difficult conversations, embrace conflict, and hold contradictory views in order to synthesize them. These are all characteristics of transformative knowers.

The deep dive is limited by the developmental capacity of the adults in schools. If a school is primarily an instrumental place, then the specific content and concrete process of the Common Theory will be attractive and hard to resist. Deeper dives ask schools to take a more self-authoring or even transformative approach. If the adult capacity does not exist, then leaders might consider strategies and deep dives that develop such capacity.

In sum, the deeper the dive, the more the turn questions cultural assumptions, spurs anxiety, makes reinvention possible, and requires adult-learning capacity, as conceptualized in Figure 5.2.

WHY IS THIS SO HARD?

If nothing else, change of any sort in schools is difficult and often results in only superficial reform. The Common Theory offers a clear, straightforward, and easily understood approach, while a deep dive of the Un-Common Theory disturbs powerful cultural forces, causes feelings of anxiety and instability, and requires a level of adult development difficult to support and sustain in many schools. The deeper the dive into school transformation or reinvention, the more is required of the school community and its leaders. It's hard work, and it has to be done well to succeed.

In the next chapter, we turn to a discussion of the strategies, tools, concepts, plans, and approaches used by schools and school leaders that have taken the deepest of dives and begun to turn toward enacting a new but not fully formed future.

CHAPTER 6

Turning
In Practice

If I could give advice to someone just starting deep change: it is ridiculously difficult. It's so hard not to cave. Often it would be easier to pretend to be someone else when you walk in the building, but how sad that would be if you were here for a reason and you lose sight of that reason. I think you only have proud moments in this work if you never lose sight of your reason for being.

—Cathy O'Connell

How did Cathy O'Connell (Chapter 5) manage this "ridiculously difficult" and risky work of turning from what was known and familiar to a less certain future? What did Matt Underwood (Chapter 5) do "when class and race rear its ugly head?" How did Deb Holman (Chapter 2) manage the "deep dive into some stuff that is tougher, and really about adults, a lot more about adults, instruction, and school culture?" How did Andres Lopez go about creating a Mexican American Literature course and helping his school rethink curriculum and student engagement in way that "wasn't threatening, but that got them to think a little differently about what they do on a daily basis?" What strategies, approaches, and practices did these leaders employ?

As we described in previous chapters, a deep dive requires (1) surfacing, exploring, shaping, and even reinventing some of the fundamental assumptions of a school's culture, (2) developing adult and organizational capacity to perform such complicated, risky work, and (3) living with and managing the personal and organizational anxiety that accompanies turning from the familiar present to a largely unknown future. The turn of the deep dive is where the uncertain future starts to be enacted. As daunting as this work is, in this chapter we discuss practices and strategies that leaders have used to navigate the turn.

SHAPING CULTURE

Cathy O'Connell and all of our school leaders would agree that "never [losing] sight of your reason for being" is the most effective strategy available to a leader and a school. Never losing your reason for being is not about visible artifacts such as schedules or textbooks, or even espoused values like mission statements or guiding principles. Rather, it is about maintaining clarity about the fundamental assumptions that you, the faculty, the school organization actually hold and act upon, assumptions about educator identity, the purpose of schooling, and issues of race, class, and power. The reason it is tempting to "pretend to be someone else" is that exposing, examining, and shaping culture always challenges widely and deeply held values and beliefs and releases anxiety throughout the organization. This "ridiculously difficult" and risky work requires (1) keeping a consistent and persistent focus, (2) wisely allocating resources, and (3) teaching and learning culture.

Consistent and Persistent Focus

At Atlanta Charter Neighborhood School the time was ripe to take on a deep dive. The school enjoyed skilled and stable leadership and faculty. Yet Matt Underwood understood that it would be easy for the focus and urgency to slip away. Few organizations embrace deep cultural change, and Matt knew it. He saw his role as keeping the sense of urgency that "we've got to do this . . . . We need to do something to create more diverse and inclusive schools, and there will be things that are challenging for us." And while he consistently promoted and communicated this message, he also worried that "we'll lose focus in some way because something else will come along [to distract us]. We're a pretty stable leadership team, but if any one of us leaves, things could be very different."

Matt had a long list of possible—and typical—distractions: "Things could change in the policy environment. Or personal issues could happen that make it easy to lose focus. Or people can just get tired." Matt understood that organizations are eager to embrace distractions to deep cultural change simply because it is demanding and produces anxiety and unease. "We're going to have to keep this focus and continue to engage teachers, parents, and whomever else we need to."

A tenacious and consistent focus on their ultimate goal was also apparent at North Reading Middle School. Michael Maloney, the assistant principal, shared: "Keeping focus is critical. It's easy to lose it and to let it go. I think Cathy [O'Connell, the principal] has been very determined. I think that her message is, 'this is what we're doing, and we are steadily working, persevering toward it, not losing the focus of where we want to go, and this is what we're going to do and this is how we're going to

---

ANDRES LOPEZ'S STORY 4: TURNING

Andres came to the school with a clear vision and a commitment to realizing it.

When I came back to my district, after I got my master's degree in literature, I knew that it was difficult to find teachers with a master's degree who wanted to teach high school. I came in wanting to be on a Title I campus, and I said to every interviewer and principal that I wanted to be in a place where I can make change. Wherever I end up, I want it to be somewhere where the department head and the administrative leadership support my endeavor to build a Mexican American Literature class.

---

do it.'" School leaders like these understand that there necessarily will be distractions in the turn. As Michael states, "It's a lot. It's a lot of work, but it's holding on to that ultimate goal, that is the key."

Matt, Cathy, and Michael understood the necessity and challenge of "holding on to that ultimate goal." They also understood that the goals addressed by the deepest dives are very different from the more linear, mechanistic goals of the Common Theory. The goals of the deepest dives produce more anxiety and unease, are challenging and risky to undertake. There is no clear path, and most of all, the deepest dives are personal. These dives question who educators are, what they value, and how they understand the world.

The deepest dives challenge educators' "reason for being" and the "reason for being" of their schools. They demand that each person examine beliefs, assumptions, and practices that they have relied on and found success with, in order to create a more robust, inclusive, and defendable array of beliefs and practices to guide future actions (Mezirow, 2000). Educators who lead deep dives understand the effort that holding on to their "reason for being" requires.

Matt and Cathy's deeply personal commitment to a yet-to-be-realized ideal helped them consistently and persistently maintain the focus needed for these deepest of dives. Yet, while maintaining focus is an essential element of the turn, that focus has to be fashioned into concrete organizational structures.

Wisely Allocating Resources

At both NRMS and ANCS, the schools' leaders allocated significant resources to support their deep dives. They made choices that were clear to the entire school community. Time was the most valuable factor in both schools. At ANCS, Matt described multiple occasions when time was allocated to building professional capacity among faculty, the leadership

---

ANDRES LOPEZ'S STORY 5: TURNING

Andres held on to his goal as he searched for ways to ease the anxiety of colleagues and lessen distractions.

If I'm building this elective, Mexican American Literature, what's going to happen? Other teachers are going to say, "What about this elective? Why don't we have this elective?" They have a point. One of the hardest things for me is when I'm going around selling the Mexican American Literature course and other students say, "What about this (another course)?" I say, "Yes, we should have that. Let your decision makers know that we need that." I knew that was going to happen. I didn't want to be against it, but I also wanted to protect the class. I didn't want it to be, "Well, the department chair is that guy's friend and that's why he has this elective." Because that is what will happen. Especially if it's a risk or an experiment, you want to protect it as much as possible. Data is not going to be enough. I told the department chair, "For this to be fair, everyone submits an elective they want to teach and we put it front of all students that would likely take electives. We get data. If none of the kids pick it, it's not meant to be here at our school. I'll do it somewhere else down the road. Just know that that's something I'm going to do at some point in my career." I said, "But if enough students pick it, now we have this information that says students want it." That was the first piece. We got that information. Enough students wanted it. Then we went on to convince counselors and administrators.

---

team, board members, and the parent community. The school also budgeted money to engage three external facilitators who were skilled in supporting conversations about race and equity. They worked initially with the leadership team and then with the entire faculty, board, and other stakeholders. Likewise at NRMS, Cathy devoted significant time to engaging faculty members in observing, exploring, reflecting, and questioning. Different members of the leadership team visited other middle schools, examined research on best practice, and studied different methods of organizing students for effective and equitable instruction. Cathy also set aside time for faculty input, parent forums, and school committee presentations. Notes from the NRMS leadership team were posted in the teacher's lounge, and teachers were invited to write questions and comments.

More broadly, NRMS leaders Cathy and Michael budgeted time in an early effort to promote adult collaboration. "We increased the collaboration times so teachers could better plan with their grade-level colleagues around best practices: Teachers were encouraged to share strategies and experiences—'What are you doing? How does that work?' It was great that we did that. Those were easy changes, but they were important because they helped get people out of their classrooms by themselves and talking with each other."

Cathy and Matt were clear about their "reason for being" in the deep dive, and they understood that a commitment to fundamental change is of minimal value without a focused allocation of resources to support it. They not only wisely allocated resources, but also allocated resources so a new, more collaborative culture could be learned.

Teaching and Learning Culture

After almost a year of diving into and observing North Reading Middle School's culture, Cathy thought the school was ready to take the next step in visualizing the emerging future. Building on the insights gained in their dive, she constructed a model that reflected that learning in order to make the school's curricular and instructional practices more equitable.

Like all good teachers, Cathy understood that complicated learning happens most effectively when the learning is situated in a schema or context (Bransford, Brown, & Cocking, 2000). She explained, "I think I felt I needed to put it out there. I thought it was time, based on the calendar, but also based on what I sensed the teams were saying to me: 'Okay we've been doing this for a while now, we'd like some tangible product of our work.'"

Putting forth a draft model was an important step in visualizing the emerging future. The faculty saw it as Cathy's job to offer a model—not a final product. Cathy speculated, "They were probably a little afraid and sort of expected 'You're the principal, Cathy, at some point you've got to grab hold and say this is what we're going to do.'" This was the beginning of the turn and an initial step into the future.

At Atlanta Neighborhood Charter School, Matt engaged in teaching of a different type. He shared that his typical response to most issues is a logical one, but through his own learning and coaching he came to realize the importance of communicating his personal commitment. As emphasized throughout this book, deep dives are highly personal, and like all good teachers, Matt understood that "personal stories from your own experiences are a way to relate . . . to call people to action and to help people understand why this work is important." Complex learning is more fully supported when it is connected to the learners' lives, when they can see and feel a personal connection (Carter, 2017). Matt further explains:

> I think in the past, I was relying just on logical arguments. I'm a pretty logical person, so I'm always trying to make the case of why we need to do something in a logical way, using data. But I've been trying more to use my own personal experiences, from my childhood and my teaching experience to frame some of the work that we're doing.

Matt is arguing that mechanistic Common Theory methods are insufficient because the deepest of dives is personal. He clarified and personalized the "reason for being" as a way for the school, faculty, and community to dare to dive into an uncertain but emerging future. He concludes, "I think that sharing my personal commitment helps to keep us focused on the personal work that is required."

Whatever strategy they used, Matt and Cathy paid consistent and persistent attention to the equity goal of their deep dives. Consistency is potent; it is what people notice, comment on, commit to, and take action around. If consistency lags or focus shifts, members of the organization are left to wonder about what is really important to the leader, how committed the leader is to the effort, and if the risk and effort to undertake a deep dive is worth the effort (Kegan et al., 2016).

DEVELOPING EXTERNAL CAPACITY

Leadership in the turn involves developing adult and organizational capacity to perform complicated and risky work. This leadership involves not only building internal organizational capacity (discussed in Chapters 4 and 5), but also working to build external capacity.

Building Political Will

Atlanta Neighborhood Charter School could not meet its economic and racial diversity goals solely by advocating for change and using internal resources. Working with his board and leadership team, Matt set out to build and expand external resources that could help ensure the school's success. They adopted two strategies designed to build broad political support. The first strategy was to expand the ANCS enrollment area to include a more diverse neighborhood. After doing so, the school built a relationship with the community engagement director of a neighborhood housing development and through that relationship launched a campaign to recruit families to ANCS. But as Matt explained, it was not sufficient to expand their population area. More had to be done.

The second involved public policy. The school had a limited number of seats available to new students annually. These were allocated through a lottery. In order to increase the odds that students from more diverse neighborhoods could successfully enroll, Matt worked to change state law to allow charter schools to use weighted lotteries to recruit more diverse student populations. He shared:

As a result of our work to change state law, ANCS is going to be the first charter school in the state to have a student enrollment

---

ANDRES LOPEZ'S STORY 6: TURNING

Building external capacity for Andres meant using social media to build political will.

Strategically, I used crowdsourcing to get money for books for the Mexican American Literature class. I knew that I could probably ask 20 friends for money and I would be able to order books, but I also wanted it to be an opportunity to say, "Hey, this class exists. It's the first of its kind." And give people a chance to be a part of it. That's how I ordered the first set of books and how I've sustained it.

---

lottery weighted to favor students whose families self-identify as being economically disadvantaged through qualifying for federal assistance, free and reduced-price lunch, or another federal economic eligibility benefit.

In order to create a broader political base to support the weighted lottery mechanism, Matt began to "work with a couple of other charter schools and the local state representative to get a change in state law to allow charter schools to have this option [to have weighted lotteries]. It just took effect, and we're the first school taking advantage of it. We are using it to impact our economic diversity." Collectively these strategies increased the political will for deep change. Political will, in combination with professional capacity and financial resources, creates what McDonald (2014) calls "action space," a critical concept for understanding the turning phase of the deep dive.

Creating an Action Space

McDonald and a group of colleagues (2014) studied large-scale efforts at deep change that happened in the 1990s in cities such as Philadelphia, Houston, and New York. The study suggests that the deepest of dives into school change requires three elements: (1) political will, (2) financial resources, and (3) professional capacity. The existence of these elements creates a space that allows deep change to occur and increases the odds that it will be sustained.

According to McDonald (2014), advocating for more inclusive, justifiable, and equitable practices is not sufficient for success. If the community and political leadership does not have the will to manage the anxiety that deep change produces, then nothing substantial will happen. Moreover, if there are limited financial resources to support the work then the change will not be sustained. Finally, as discussed in Chapters 3 and 4, when the organization has not developed the professional capacity for complex

---

ANDRES LOPEZ'S STORY 7: TURNING

Andres was aware that political will is a powerful and necessary tool.

I said to administrators, "I don't need you to make it happen. I just need you to be on my side, so that I can make it happen." I was ready to do that. I capitalized on the fact that they needed and wanted me and I had commitment from them. Then I built support. I said, "OK, my buy-in is great. Admin's buy-in is great. I need teacher buy-in. I need student buy-in. Because again, it's political.

---

thinking, resisting easy answers, considering a variety of perspectives, or embracing an unknown future, then the deep dive will be shallow at best, perhaps with no turn at all. If any of the three elements of the action space are missing or diminished, the deep dive and, more specifically, the turn is not likely to produce sustainable results (McDonald, 2014). Figure 6.1 summarizes the idea of action space.

Both Cathy and Matt worked to create an action space to support their deep dive and turn. They budgeted money especially for time for more collaboration and resources such as external facilitators, retreats, and professional learning opportunities. Moreover, Cathy and Matt, as well as all the leaders in this book, focused on adult development as a way to build the professional capacity needed for the complicated work required by a deep dive. In each case, leaders spent considerable time, money, and attention to develop the "intellectual, technical, and organizational know-how available to sustain a creative and accountable teaching and learning community" (McDonald, 2014, p. 23).

Political will—or civic capacity—is one of most neglected sides of the action space triangle. As McDonald (2014) describes it, *civic capacity* is the "extent to which various sections of the community understand, support, and actively contribute to reform" (p. 23). Community might include civic groups, nonprofit organizations, professional and governmental groups, and, particularly, "those people in a direct line of impact—notably parents and students" (p. 23).

Like ANCS, North Reading Middle School built civic support with both external and internal community members. As Cathy explains,

I had tremendous support from my superintendent. But I was worried about the community's response. My scheduled presentation of our initial model got snowed out three times, but finally I did present it to the school committee along with the superintendent. The superintendent joined me in discussing the changes with the school community, and we asked for their endorsement, which they gave.

Figure 6.1. Action Space

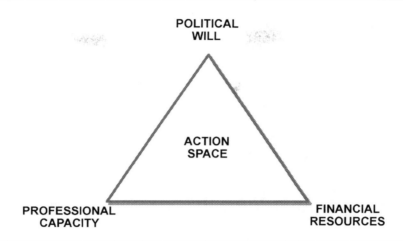

POLITICAL
WILL

ACTION
SPACE

PROFESSIONAL
CAPACITY

FINANCIAL
RESOURCES

Note. Adapted from *American School Reform: What Works, What Fails, and Why* (p. 23), by J. P. McDonald, 2014, Chicago, IL: University of Chicago Press.

Because Cathy had involved the superintendent from the first, created a broad-based leadership team of teachers and parents, held open houses for parents, devoted faculty meetings to the new structures, and kept the school committee informed, the pushback from the community was more limited than Cathy had initially feared. She shared, "I think I received two or three phone calls from parents." Her attention to political will increased the possibility the new structure would be effective and sustainable. No turn happens without a robust action space.

MANAGING ANXIETY

Change causes unease, releases anxiety, increases worry, and produces discomfort. This is because schools, like most organizations, are conservative places (Hargreaves & Shirley, 2009; Lortie, 1975). Even the changes that come with the Common Theory—textbook adoptions, new programs, and fresh curriculum—can cause considerable unease. The deep dive into fundamental assumptions, emerging futures, and contentious subjects such as race, power, equity, or the purpose of schools causes even greater anxiety and discomfort. It cannot be avoided. In Chapter 5, we conceptualized the idea that the deeper the dive, the more anxiety in the organization (as shown in Figure 6.2).

One of the most significant—and loneliest—roles leaders assume in a deep dive is managing the anxiety that is released, their own and that of

Figure 6.2. The Anxiety Produced by the Deep Dive

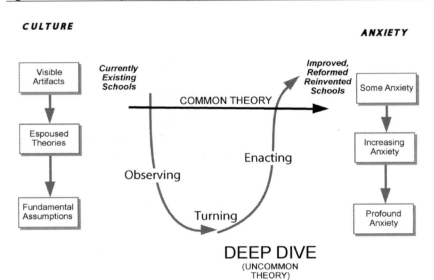

the organization (Heifetz et al., 2009). Anxiety affects every aspect of the school community—parents, students, faculty, policymakers, sometimes even neighbors. It also affects the leader. The better able a leader is to manage the tension associated with change, the more likely the organization, individuals in the organization, and the leader will not only survive the turn toward the future but embrace it. Just as the leader provides support for the organization and individuals, a leader must build a personal support system of individuals and groups he or she can call on for both coaching as well as reassurance during the turn of any deep dive.

How Leaders Manage Their Own Anxiety in the Turn

Leaders who lead the deepest dives have to manage the tension, unease, and anxiety in the organization, and the same things in themselves. Heifetz et al. (2009) tells us, "People who lead adaptive change most successfully have a diagnostic mind-set about themselves as well as about the situation. That is, they are continually striving to understand what is going on inside, how they are changing over time, and how they as a system interact with their organization as a system" (p. 184). Leaders are not separate from the organizations they lead, the culture holds them as well. The personal and organizational tension needs to be managed.

School leaders who successfully navigate the turn of the deep dive often employ four practices to manage tension and anxiety as the work

---

ANDRES LOPEZ'S STORY 8: TURNING

Like other leaders, Andres reached out to allies, including university colleagues, for support.

I had to deal with a lot of misconceptions. I said, "Mexican American Literature," and then some English teachers would start mentioning authors that were from different Latin American countries. They weren't understanding Mexican American as its own thing. And there weren't books for a class like this yet and not even a curriculum for this in high school. I had to capitalize on what exists at the university level, partner with as many people that I could who do anything remotely like this, like other ethnic studies in high school classes, Mexican American Literature and Mexican American Studies in college classes, and others to build a group of allies.

---

deepens: (1) get out of the school, (2) take an inquiry approach toward the turn, (3) find thought partners, and (4) use an external coach/mentor/ facilitator in the process.

Get Out of the School. At ANCS, Matt Underwood cultivated both formal and informal connections with like-minded educators. He explains,

> I read a book a few years ago about habits of savvy leaders. One of the recommendations was something like go to conferences, because in your role, rarely do you have someone that's in the same position as you at the school. Conferences offer a chance to talk about ideas. I try to do that a couple of times each year, and I feel guilty, but I also know that getting out of this bubble in which I work is really important.

Moreover, Matt has long been a part of the Coalition of Essential Schools (see website at essentialschools.org), and ANCS embraces its principles. Yet, as he began this deep dive into equity, he sought out diverse schools as well. Recently, he became connected to an informal group of schools committed to thinking deeply about equitable schools. He explained, "There are charter schools out there that are trying to be intentionally diverse, seeking to have a 50/50 in terms of race or economic status. Through this organization I have been able to connect with them about what works for them, what's challenging. It has really been beneficial." Matt understood how important it is to get out of his school and office and connect with educators facing the same issues.

Take an Inquiry Approach. At NRMS Cathy shared a similar opinion about the importance of professional learning for herself and Michael, the assistant principal. "I think we were able to create our own professional development as principals. I think you can become isolated and distant from the work, and just charge along thoughtlessly if you're not continuing to grow professionally yourself." Both Cathy and Michael were enrolled in part-time graduate school leadership programs and used opportunities offered by their coursework to expand their knowledge and skill in leading deep change. The focus of Cathy's doctoral dissertation was the change she was leading at the school. Similarly, Michael focused his graduate research on their efforts.

Find Thought Partners. Matt also sought support and coaching by reaching out to trusted colleagues.

> I definitely try to call upon those people when I have an idea, or a question, or just need someone to talk me off the ledge. I've got different individuals for different types of questions. There's a group of school leaders through that National Coalition of Diverse Charter Schools I've talked with more and more over the past year. And on occasion I talk over the phone or exchange email with a longtime trusted colleague. I also talk through ideas and issues with external facilitators we engage in the school. And then my wife too, she knows the community so well. She taught here for a couple of years, and she knows about schooling and being in school. I often call on a range of people.

Cathy and Michael also sought out thought partners in the various networks that they were part of. Cathy was part of a Leadership Critical Friends Group (Fahey, 2012) and Michael's graduate program used a cohort model he relied on. However, their most important partners were each other. Cathy said, "We have each other, thank goodness. It makes all the difference. You cannot do this work alone."

Use an External Coach/Mentor/Facilitator. Both Cathy and Matt used external coaches and facilitators. Matt understood that he might not have the facilitation skills to lead difficult conversations about race, and besides, he also needed to be part of the conversations. He needed to be able to step out of his role as head of school to be a learner and struggle with these thorny issues as well. Consequently, Matt hired facilitators to engage the leadership team and faculty in racial and economic equity work.

Cathy and Michael used a consultant/facilitator to act as a sounding board for their thinking and to facilitate NRMS 2.0. Cathy explains: "It was important to have a consultant so we could participate as team members; not trying to run the meeting, but able to listen and learn all at the same time." Cathy, Michael, and Matt all expressed the same idea: Create space to be a learner, struggle along with the community with problematic issues, and sit with difficult questions.

In general, school leaders who successfully navigate a turn through deep change agree on one important idea: Don't do this work alone. Don't retreat to your office and think up great things for others to do, don't be afraid of not knowing, and don't be uncomfortable with questions. In short, leaders manage the tensions of the work of the turn by creating room to be both leaders and learners. The emerging future has to be learned by everyone.

How Leaders Support Others in the Turn

Engaging in a yearlong conversation—listening, responding, modeling, teaching, and coaching—were among the many practices that Cathy and Michael used to support faculty through the deep dive at NRMS. The support didn't end when they shared the initial draft model but continued. Cathy explains,

> We took time to get input. We did a lot of debriefing at faculty meetings. "This is what we're thinking about, this is what we're planning. What are three things you're worried about?" or "What are some questions that you have?" We were good about getting that back to them. We wrote responses to all of the questions everybody had, answering the ones that we felt that we could.

Not only did they meet with the whole faculty, they also met with grade-level teams and individuals, always communicating the shared goal of eliminating leveling but also coaching, teaching, and responding to questions and concerns.

What was important about Cathy and Michael's practice was that they continued the conversation. They understood that not every concern would be addressed or question answered about a future that did not yet exist, but they persistently reassured everyone that the conversation and the learning about the new future would continue. As Michael describes it, "We've encouraged people. Good teachers—for whatever reasons, either they don't have time or they don't want to or no one has even asked them—often have not looked for different ways of doing things. But we are having that conversation." And, like Matt, they emphasized that throughout it all, what matters most is "what's best for the kids." With every decision, the question is asked, "Who is it the best for?" "Providing interventions for kids, it's best for kids. Not leveling kids, it's best for kids. Conversations among and with teachers, because it's best for kids."

At ANCS there were multiple structures in place to support teachers as they turned into school reinvention. As they entered the crucial turn toward the future, Matt reflected, "I feel my job is to help get teachers, especially, through this process feeling they are agents of their own change and that we can do this work together." Like Cathy and Michael, Matt understood that the new future had to be learned and that the school had to do that learning together.

> We're going to work collaboratively to figure out the best ways to support a diverse community. While there are probably some things that we're doing now that we'll do differently or not at all in 2, 3, 4 years through this work, there are other things like the core CES [Coalition of Essential Schools] principles that are going to be the same. That's what I'm trying to emphasize, while at the same time keeping that sense of urgency that we've got to do this. We need to do this, and there will be some things that are going to be challenging.

Cathy, Michael, and Matt navigated the turn by resisting the prescriptions and formulas of the Common Theory. They talked about "continuing the conversation," "learning together," "being agents of their own change," and "encouraging people." Schein (2016) describes how deep change happens only when an organization diminishes its learning anxiety and builds the capacity of the organization for complex learning. Cathy, Michael, and Matt understood that as their schools became better at learning together, learning anxiety would decrease and their schools could dive deeper into a new future. In Matt's words, "the learning is tough, but we will do it together."

A FINAL WORD ABOUT TURNING

Leading a school into and through the perilous turn of a deep dive demands skill, support, knowledge, and courage. In this chapter we offer some practices that can help and have shared the stories of how two schools used them. And while making a deep dive and turning toward a still emerging future may be dangerous, it also offers great possibility. As Donald Schön reminds us,

> Under circumstances in which you have the creation of a community of reliable inquiry, capable of drawing on multiple sources of knowledge and upon multiple sources of intuition, in a context in which something is at stake, and our worry is how to take action, with a sense that we *have*

to take action, and that there is a *we* here trying to do this. Under *those* circumstances there is greatest ground for hope. (McDonald, 2014, p. 28)

And, in the end, it can occur. Cathy shares:

We did exactly what we said we were going to do, we invited anybody to participate, we updated them along the way. We said we're going to look at what we do, we're going to visit other schools, we're going to read research, we're going to talk, we're going to report back to you. But in the end our goal is to make recommendations for change with the essential question of "How can we better meet the needs of our students today and tomorrow?" And we did just that.

CHAPTER 7

Enacting
The Third Phase of the Deep Dive

School improvement happens in one year, but school transformation,
that doesn't happen in one year.

—Deirdre Williams

When Deirdre Williams, former principal of Attucks Middle School
in Houston, Texas, began her work there, it was considered a "failing"
school. This identity was not only held by district and state officials but
also permeated the attitudes and behaviors of the teachers, students, and
community. Students who lived in the neighborhood, and who could
do so, opted to leave Attucks to go to other district magnet schools. The
mobility rate was high. Deirdre realized she didn't know the school and
needed answers to two questions: "Why am I losing all these kids?" And
"Where are they going?" These questions led the school into a deep dive
as it began engaging in the observing phase we highlighted in Chapters
3 and 4.

During her first year, Deirdre visited more than 65 churches in the
area, trying to understand the community and what it would take to bring
students and their families back to their neighborhood school. To build
a better understanding of their students and the issues they were facing, faculty members began home visits. The school held gender-specific,
student–faculty assemblies that allowed students to ask questions on their
minds that they may not have asked in a mixed-gender group. Deirdre
described the process as "starting to build relationships and help everyone
to become human."

Deirdre discovered that many in the community and school thought
that Attucks "was never intended to be for exceptionally performing kids.
There were other schools in the area for those high-performing kids. Attucks was a place to house those students who were not going to get
in somewhere else." Enrichment programs did not exist, and the only
special academic programs were for math or reading remediation, with
no regard to whether students needed or wanted other opportunities for
extending their learning.

But that was not the vision Deirdre held for the school: "I didn't have a vision for us to be some remediation school. The kids deserved more than that. I saw another picture for the kids in that community. I went with the picture I saw, and we began to work." Thus began the deep dive at Attucks, as Deirdre led the faculty, community, and students to begin "to imagine the worlds of our hopes" to reach toward "not what is but what is to become" (Gergen, 2014, p. 294).

ENACTING THE FUTURE AT ATTUCKS MIDDLE SCHOOL

Deirdre knew that the work of their dive required that they confront the inequity inherent in the structures and practices of the school. They uncovered and challenged assumptions and built capacity to look at their current and past practices and how they perpetuated the environment of failure. Deirdre and the leadership team engaged the faculty in multiple professional development experiences. They challenged the prevailing culture by establishing routines to shape a new one. For example, when Deirdre first arrived, classrooms were often chaotic. Since it was common-place for disruptive students to be sent out of class or suspended, students were often unsupervised in the hallways. Suspension rates were rising. One of the first actions Deirdre took was to put in place systems to help establish order and relationships. Students could no longer be suspended or sent out of class for minor infractions. Instead, leadership team members regularly visited classrooms and offered teachers classroom management feedback and suggestions. They instituted regular phone calls and face-to-face conferences with families. Administrators moved their desks into hallways so they were visible and accessible to students, teachers, and community members.

At the end of the first year, Deirdre recommended that only 18 of the 35 faculty members return to the school. As she explained, "I kept hearing 'these kids.' I didn't hear the language of 'our kids' or 'my kids.'" The original plan was to do a lot of professional development, or put in place programs, and other such things—the work of the Common Theory. But then it occurred to Deirdre, "I can teach you all this, but if you don't even believe the kids are worthy of any of it, I've just wasted my money. I don't think any of us can grow as students, teachers, and leaders until we have something that tells us that we have the capacity to do so." They needed to go deeper.

Guided by a commitment to equity and excellence for all students and a belief in a better future, Deirdre, the returning and newly hired faculty members, and the administrative team set out to create a better version of their school, one more aligned with their new vision. This became manifest when they learned that the community had long wanted

a STEM (science technology engineering and mathematics) program at
the school, but neither the district nor community leaders believed the
students had the potential or ability. In their second year, Deirdre wrote
grants to establish a STEM academy. Deirdre and the school were embracing the thorniest and hardest of issues of equity and excellence.

ENACTING THE FUTURE AT BARROW ELEMENTARY SCHOOL

At Barrow Elementary School in Athens, Georgia, Andy Plemmons
strived to engage students in authentic learning experiences, initially as
a classroom teacher and then as head of the library media center. When
he first moved into the library media center, he embraced current and
emerging technologies to build on students' interests and create platforms
for more accessible, authentic, and engaging learning. While he started in
his role as a media specialist with some ideas and practices in place, over
time his thinking about how the library might become a center of teaching and learning grew. Andy began to push against existing boundaries of
commonly held notions of teaching and learning.

One summer, after participating in several professional learning experiences with library media colleagues from across the country, Andy decided that it was time to take on the fundamental reinvention of teaching
and learning experiences that students were having in the library media
center and across the school. In previous collaboration with teachers, he
noticed the extent to which they did and didn't provide authentic, meaningful learning for every student. He noticed which students were engaged
and successful, and which were not. He became increasingly frustrated as
he saw limited student learning and limited teacher collaboration. He was
convinced it was time to move beyond traditional thinking and reinvent
teaching and learning. He was ready for the hard work of a deep dive.
Like the other leaders in this book, Andy reached out to others to develop political capacity and support. He initially auditioned his ideas and
vision with library and technology specialists through a blog and social
media. After reading Andy's blog, the Barrow Elementary School principal invited Andy to talk with her about his ideas. As a result of their conversation, time was allocated during the fall preplanning days for Andy
to meet with each grade-level team in the building. This was a key first
step in creating the internal capacity to support the success of the dive.
These meetings were the first of many in which Andy and his colleagues
shared and explored their ideas and experiences in teaching and learning
and began to imagine a riskier, less-known approach in which students
became cocreators of their own learning. Andy explained, "It made such
a difference to have that time in the beginning of the year to talk with
teachers and help them understand that I was willing to take a risk with

them to try something that we hadn't tried before, and not know really what the end product would be."

While some teachers and teams were hesitant to imagine a different vision, the seed was planted, and the turn to the future began. Not only did Andy move forward in creating and trying out prototypes within the media center, he also attracted teacher colleagues who wanted to join him in taking the risks of co-reinventing an unknown future. Chapter 8 describes the Barrow Peace Prize, one of the many prototypes that Andy and his colleagues created that became a nationally recognized student project embodying the power of student voice.

> There are so many requirements that come from the state and from the district that cause you to be in a box. You get put on timelines. You have certain assessments that have to be done and certain procedures that you have to follow. There's a scope and sequence that says everybody's supposed to be in the same place at the same time.
>
> —Andy Plemmons

ENACTING AND REALIZING THE DIMENSIONS OF CULTURE, CAPACITY, AND ANXIETY

This chapter is about the work that comes after the turn. We call this phase "enacting" because it is about en-acting—acting out, acting on—what you now know you must do and why for the better, more equitable future that you are trying to realize. After observing, uncovering, and disturbing fundamental assumptions, this final phase of the deep dive is about trying out (i.e., enacting) new ideas, structures, and prototypes based on new assumptions. Table 7.1 summarizes how culture, capacity, and anxiety work in this phase and the two previous phases.

For Deirdre, it meant that the school had to confront its inequitable past practices and enact new ones based on the new assumption that the students, teachers, school, and community could be successful. In Andy's case, it was about enacting practices that embodied the new assumption that individual students could be fuller participants in and designers of their own learning.

Enacting employs the internal and external capacity built into the observing and turning phases of the dive to support a new future. As Scharmer (2006) shares, "my most important insight has been that there are *two different* sources of learning: learning from experiences of the *past* and learning from the *future* as it emerges" (p. 5).

The enacting phase is not the search for and implementation of the perfect plan or solution—seeking a "best practice" or program that is manageable with predetermined processes and outcomes would be the Common Theory approach. The enacting phase is a lot messier and riskier. It

Table 7.1 How Culture, Capacity, and Anxiety Manifest in the Three Phases of the Deep Dive

Dimension	Phase 1: Observing	Phase 2: Turning	Phase 3: Enacting
Culture	Uncovering, observing, exploring, letting go	Disturbing, shaping	Trying on, realizing, enacting and co-enacting
Capacity: Internal and External	Focus on internal: building capacity through adult development	Focus on external: action space	Using and employing the capacity
Anxiety	Raising and managing: internal (personal and organizational)	Holding	Diminishing and using

is about classrooms, schools, or organizations learning their way toward better selves, the work of the UnCommon Theory. Enacting is about tackling the thorniest issues, not with talk or historical analyses, but instead with prototypes to test out ideas and generate feedback so that educators are continually learning and refining. Enacting is not setting up pilots and then implementing them on a wider scale. It is getting to the place of action in the deep dive and using cycles of small prototypes through which educators continue to learn by and through the doing.

An UnCommon Theory must counteract the "conservatism, isolationism, and presentism" described in Chapter 1 that characterizes schools and supports the Common Theory (Hargreaves & Shirley, 2009; Lortie, 1975). The enacting phase of the dive builds on the internal skill and capacity developed in the observing phase, and the will and capacity developed in the turning phase. Schein (2016) reminds us that "leaders can change what they pay attention to, control, and reward" (p. 237). In the enacting phase, leaders pay attention to moving forward. They counter conservatism with innovation through prototyping, isolationism with collective capacity and building on relationships, and presentism with a future-forward orientation.

In the next section, we will take a look at each of these ways to enact.

UTILIZING STRATEGIES FOR ENACTING THE FUTURE

Gergen (2014) said, "The best way to predict the future is to create it" (p. 294). Both Deirdre and Andy envisioned a future in which every student had opportunities to engage in challenging, quality learning that mattered both for them and for a larger community. More important, they set out to achieve it. They both engaged in cycles of enacting through prototyping, refining, and continuous effort to build collective capacity. These three strategies build on the fundamental principles of improvement science (Bryk, Gomez, Grunow, & LeMahieu, 2015) and appreciative inquiry (Cooperrider & Whitney, 2005; Gergen, 2014; Tschannen-Moran & Clement, 2018). They are utilized by leaders and the collective community to envision and enact a future that might be more "liberatory, practice producing, and action centered" (Gergen, 2014, p. 303).

Learning by Doing: Improvement Science

Learning to improve and learning by doing are central tenets of improvement science (Bryk et al., 2015). Some core improvement questions include: "What is the specific problem I am trying to solve? What change might I introduce and why? And, how will I know if the change is actually an improvement?" (Bryk et al., 2015, p. 9).

This approach builds on educators' ongoing practice of introducing new approaches in their classrooms and schools and emphasizes deliberate and systematic analysis of the outcomes. Bryk and colleagues (2015) emphasize that educators are not research "users"—they are active "improvers" who look at specific problems and evidence in small cycles, called PDSA cycles (plan, do, study, act). As these "subsequent cycles of redesign and testing unfold, a better understanding evolves of the actual problem or problems that need to be solved and more workable interventions begin to emerge" (p. 9).

Deirdre and the leadership team at Attucks used this process of plan, do, study, act when they engaged in multiple cycles of observing classroom instruction to assess needs. They planned and conducted mini professional learning experiences with classroom coaching, and they enacted PDSA cycles to look at teachers' questions about teaching and learning in learning communities.

Improvement science suits this part of the dive because it avoids the Common Theory pitfalls. This process of disciplined inquiry emphasizes "learning fast to implement well" as opposed to "going fast and learning slow" (Bryk et al., 2015, p. 7). Educators design and implement cycles of redesign and testing knowing that each cycle will get closer to better questions and better actions. Because educators usually work in familiar contexts to solve familiar, longstanding, and well-ingrained challenges, they need new ways of looking at their context's particular opportunities and challenges. Improvement science provides new perspectives. Without working hard to understand contexts, neither Deirdre nor Andy could have managed their dives.

Bryk and his colleagues (2015) describe several principles that guide improvement science:

1. Make the work problem-specific and focused on the point of view of the user.
2. Focus on variation in performance to attend to "what works, for whom, and under what set of conditions?"
3. Make the complexities of the issue visible to create an "evolving framework for collective action."
4. Collect evidence that can be "easily woven into the day-to-day work of students and educators" throughout the process.
5. Attend to developing needed knowledge, building capabilities and will for change.
6. Place priority on "solving a problem together." (pp. 12–17)

Improvement science not only supports launching multiple small trials that yield evidence to learn from; it also actively engages educators as collaborators in the trying out and refining. This collaboration can increase shared ownership and responsibility in co-enacting the future.

Moving into the future, leaders do not want momentum to stall by attempting to create the "perfect" approach or one "best" way. Instead, they encourage multiple ways to look at a challenge or issue, engaging different people and perspectives in cocreating the next steps toward the future. Scharmer (2018) provides helpful imagery for this, as he calls what is being cobuilt "landing strips of the future" (p. 114). Andy and his colleagues built such landing strips by taking small steps and learning from each of them along the way. Andy explains,

> Sometimes the next step is one teacher on a team taking a risk with me, and we see where it goes. We say it's a "first go." Then we show the rest of the team what we did and ask, "Are you interested in trying it out?" I guess then it's not as risky at that point, but certainly it's going to be different the second time because we are always thinking about how to change something to make it better.

Through cocreating the next steps toward the future, the old culture is disrupted, and a new one is being cocreated. It becomes energizing to see change and learn from it. Many are involved, and ownership is shared as everyone is learning by doing. As Andy recounts,

> Having a project like this is helpful to our collaborative planning, to see what happened in a project because we gave ourselves permission to try something new. And we didn't abandon the standards we were setting out to teach. We included those and many more.

ANDRES LOPEZ'S STORY 9: ENACTING

Andres also is building landing strips to lead toward the future.

I'm always thinking in the spring about the next year. Putting new ideas [prototypes] into place and really pushing yourself can be fulfilling, otherwise you get stagnant as a teacher. I try them out in the spring, when the kids and I know each other, not at the start of the year when we don't have that trust and relationship.

Improvement science shares themes with teacher action research, design thinking, and entrepreneurship. It draws on creativity, imagination, and invention to offer a highly integrated set of methods for developing technical knowledge that helps to transform good ideas into practices that work.

Coming at It Through Success: Appreciative Inquiry

Reflecting on co-enacting at Attucks Middle School, Deirdre recounts:

> We had a lot of conversations and planning. We called it appreciative inquiry. We looked at what we did really well. Where were our scores that were solid? What did we do to get there? That really energizes people. We had some low areas, but when we talked about what we did really well, everybody was energized to do a whole lot more of what we did well so that we could address the low scores.

Once Deirdre and the leaders created a space for sharing good work, teachers began to ask each other what they were doing and how. Teachers began developing model lessons for difficult or challenging concepts and shared those by teaching, practicing, and coplanning them. The school began to understand that when teachers were learning, their students were learning.

Deirdre heard the conversation change from "my kids couldn't do this" to "I didn't teach this well"—which is a different approach. Donohoo, Hattie, and Eells (2018) describe this shift to shared language for student learning, which replaces conversations about instructional compliance, as a sign of collective efficacy.

Appreciative inquiry works from strengths, which represents both a philosophical stance and a strategy to look for, understand, and build on what appears to be working. Like improvement science, appreciative inquiry is a future-forming strategy to shape a new, unknown future (Cooperrider & Whitney, 2005; Gergen, 2014; Tschannen-Moran & Clement, 2018). It requires listening to the experiences and perspectives of colleagues, and from those stories identifying common values and strengths. From those values and strengths, new directions are developed. As Gergen (2014) describes it, "problem talk is replaced by dialogue with an appreciative focus"(p. 300).

Taking an ongoing approach brings appreciative inquiry closer to shaping and being the culture of the school rather than "something we did once." Gergen notes that the outcome of this inquiry, as opposed to more traditional approaches, "is an increasing sense that 'the best way to predict the future is to create it'" (p. 300). In Chapter 8, we describe how Deirdre and Andy went about cocreating the future they envisioned with their colleagues.

Enacting Collective Capacity

The final strategy of this phase is enacting or realizing the future through collective action and ownership. If not enacted collectively, the emerging future won't be owned and realized widely. It cannot be because the leader, consultant, or mandate said so—rather it is enacting a better future together and using the internal and external capacity they together have built.

Deirdre discovered that when the administrative team worked alongside teachers, they began to see leaders as colearners. Teachers learned that leaders, including Deirdre, were also videoing themselves, analyzing feedback, looking at school data, and asking what they could improve in their practice. "It was then that things started to shift. Learning and accountability became shared when it became transparent to teachers that leaders were being coached." Learning and practicing together built the notion that everyone was working on becoming better on behalf of the students. Deirdre credits the team: "I couldn't have done it without the team. Just the experience of getting teachers and leaders to start shifting our thought process to say, 'Wait a minute, we can do this.' Our 6th-graders started with some of the lowest scores in the district, and by 8th grade they had some of the highest."

As Scharmer (2006) reminds us, "When groups learn to operate from a real future possibility that is seeking to emerge, they begin to tap into a different social field that manifests through an altered reality of thinking, conversing, and collective action" (p. 3). This is the work of reinvention. Working on uncovering and understanding fundamental assumptions leads to better processes for observing together, turning together, and then enacting the better future together with a clearer sense of purpose and more internal capacity with external support. Bandura's 1993 research indicates that "when educators share a sense of collective efficacy, school cultures tend to be characterized by beliefs that reflect high expectation for student success" (quoted in in Donohoo et al., 2018, p. 42).

Andres Lopez's Story 10: Enacting

Andres is aware that he has to collect stories and other data of what is working in his Mexican American Literature class, and to think about how to share that learning and its effects on students and the school with multiple audiences. He also relies on the data to inform his practice, frequently prototyping in his classroom and engaging students as co-evaluators of these efforts. Sharing data and engaging students as co-enactors helped create collective capacity.

How do you know this is having an effect? It's things like seeing attendance go up. One kid, who rarely shares anything, simply but clearly said, "Last semester I always skipped my eighth period class. I come to this class every day eighth period, because when I leave the class I feel awesome." Other students were moved by her comments.

There are times where I have to activate my old macho "don't cry in front of people" skills because students share things that move me. They read something and then understand something, connect to it, or share it with their families. I didn't imagine they were going to take it home and reread something with their grandparent or their brother or their tio [uncle] and say, "Is this how it was? Can you relate to this?" I didn't expect that. Before teaching this literature, I saw kids love certain books sometimes, but I didn't always see them carrying a book close to their heart the way they do now. That's been a change and ripple effect.

I've also seen their critical eye, the way that they look at literature as having more to tell them than just the standard message that they're supposed to take away from it. I find this critical reading enhances their ability in all their classes. This is something I talk about with my colleagues across the departments.

I talked a student into taking this class, and it reinvigorated her appreciation of literature. She had left advanced courses and the college track, saying "I probably won't go to college," and now she's back to wanting to take a class her senior year, dual credit or Advanced Placement, that would put her on the trajectory to explore these subjects again in college. Hers is a common story. To have missed the chance to help her develop, that would have really broken my heart.

I also see evidence of success with students who normally have their heads down in class. I sent a picture of one particular student every day to the department head, who said early on, "That student is difficult. If he's different in this class, then I'm sold." I sent the department head pictures of every assignment that student did and pictures of the student participating in class and raising his hand. I didn't necessarily know what success would look like. I knew that there was data supporting it, but I didn't know what it was going to look like in every case.

Andres's Story, continued:

Now, I'm frustrated with how hard it has been to build on this one class. I'm happy that it's growing here at our school, but it needs to be available in a lot more schools. It should be everywhere and all over San Antonio. I'm talking to everyone every time I get a chance. Right now, it's like a flame, and it's hard to put out that flame, but the flame hasn't spread. You can still put it out.

Collective capacity is built by all phases of the deep dive. The observing and turning movements are essential for the dive to go beyond the shallows of the Common Theory approach to fundamentally reshape culture and practice. The collective power of the work done in the observing and turning phases of the deep dive comes to full bloom in this enacting phase. Bryk et al. (2015) emphasize that learning accelerates when it is undertaken in community with others. For Deirdre it was with the leadership team, faculty, and community; for Andy, with teachers and students across the school and through online communities of other educators; for Andres, with his students, colleagues, and community supporters. This type of collective action "vitalizes a core belief that we can accomplish more together than even the best of us can achieve alone" (p. 17). It is this "profound normative shift" (p. 17) through which today's challenges are better understood and better action is enacted and realized.

ENACTING A BETTER FUTURE

In this chapter we described the enacting phase of the deep dives that Deirdre and Andy undertook. A middle school principal and an elementary school library media specialist entered this phase employing three key strategies: (1) engaging in cycles of prototyping to "learn by doing," and (2) participating in appreciative inquiry into current success as a foundation for future actions, and (3) tapping into existing collective capacity while expanding it to ensure collective ownership.

In the next chapter, we describe "Enacting: In Practice— Co-Enacting." This phase necessarily requires moving from a personal commitment to shared commitment and action.

CHAPTER 8

Enacting
In Practice—Co-Enacting

You aren't just trying to think about the next step you are going to take, but thinking ten times beyond, where you shoot for the moon and see where you really end up landing.

—Andy Plemmons

As we described in Chapter 7, Andy Plemmons focused on reinventing learning and teaching at Barrow Elementary School through his leadership in the library media center. Andy could have kept "good enough" going in the library; after all, there were no complaints. It matched and probably even exceeded the image of a school library. But he knew there was more that could be done to engage each student, along with their teachers and families, in more meaningful and powerful learning. He could have worked alone on the concept of reinventing teaching and learning within the library media center, without disrupting the culture and practices beyond its walls. But he knew that such an individualistic approach ultimately would not serve his aspirations for students. Andy was also aware that the state and district in which he and his colleagues worked promoted a top-down Common Theory approach to teaching and learning that made "going along" with mandates prevalent and reinvention difficult.

CO-ENACTING A BETTER FUTURE
AT BARROW ELEMENTARY SCHOOL

During the first phase of the dive at Barrow, Andy and his colleagues met to analyze student experiences to learn what was effective and for whom. They talked about lesson plans and projects. During these conversations, Andy began to raise questions about how they might create opportunities for more student-centered, authentic, and engaging curriculum. He also posted a line from a children's book, *Flora & Ulysses* by Kate DiCamillo (2013), in the library and on his blog about expecting the miraculous.

The line says something like miraculous things happen every
day, maybe every other day, maybe every few weeks, or maybe
sometimes they don't happen at all, but we still expect that
miraculous things are going to happen. That made me think—you
can take a risk in education that things may not turn out the way
you envision it in the beginning, but if you keep your eyes open
along the way, there are really miraculous things happening all
around you. You just have to be watching, observing, and looking
for them. Maybe not looking for the thing that was going to happen,
but looking at what is actually happening.

Soon an opportunity presented itself. Andy had previously worked
with the 2nd-grade teachers on a project that required students to research historical figures, select one they thought deserved to be featured
on a postage stamp, write an essay about that person, and draw a postage
stamp to accompany their essay. The final products were displayed in the
school. The teachers designed the project and asked Andy to help them
with the research aspect. Both the project and the collaboration between
the teachers and Andy were typical of the Common Theory approach in
many schools.

However, inspired by Andy's concepts of expecting the miraculous
and moon-shot goals, which emphasized being opened to possibilities
that can emerge when students are not only consumers but also creators
of information, one of the 2nd-grade teachers approached him. Andy
explains, "She said we have this project, but we want to see where we
might go with it together." This initial interest and enthusiasm formed
the platform to launch a collaboration between Andy and the entire
2nd-grade team into co-enacting the future. Drawing on elements of
improvement science and appreciative inquiry (described in Chapter 7),
they embarked on a series of iterative cycles of creating, refining, and
trying out new versions of this reinvented traditional project. Andy and
the teachers focused on creating a more authentic project, one with
more opportunities for students to be codesigners of their learning and
to open new possibilities by sharing the projects with audiences across
the school and beyond.

The project was reinvented as the Barrow Peace Prize. It became more
authentic as students wrote a persuasive essay rather than a descriptive
report. In their essays, students had to convince others that their historical figure deserved to be awarded the prize.

Students became cocreators of their learning by developing the criteria for the prize instead of the teachers. Using Google Hangout, Andy
facilitated a simultaneous cross-classroom virtual meeting with all of the
2nd-grade students in the school. Students used the resulting criteria to
shape their persuasive essays.

ANDRES LOPEZ'S STORY 11: CO-ENACTING

By sharing his passion and ideas, Andres opened possibilities.

What happens is the passion for your idea is infectious. People really respond to this thing that you believe in, and if it's all about what is best for kids, then it's really hard for anyone to question what you're trying to do.

The project was made public. Previously, students' reports and post-age stamp renderings were posted in the school hallways, where they received limited attention, and there were few opportunities for interaction with an audience other than the 2nd-grade teachers who graded the projects. As a part of its reinvention as an UnCommon project, the students' work was shared via social media with audiences across the school, local community, and with global audiences far beyond. These diverse audiences studied the student-created criteria, read the persuasive essays, cast votes for the most deserving figures, and eventually selected the winner of the Barrow Peace Prize. Andy, the teachers, and students were co-enacting the future.

Andy also engaged the school's art teacher, who worked with the students to create art symbolizing their historic figures. Her involvement opened the experience to multiple forms of learning and creating, increased time and opportunity for expansive learning, and upended perceived constraints (i.e., the Common Theory).

Rather than predetermining the outcomes of the project, they opened it up to the possibilities that emerged, and the project blossomed and grew in unexpected ways from their collective efforts. Andy reflects, "Taking that idea and considering it through a lens of 'expecting the miraculous,' the project began to change. We didn't know what would happen along the way, but by sharing it first within the school, and then making students' work public on social media and on my blog, things began to happen." Andy, the students, and teachers had a successful first year of the Barrow Peace Prize because they were open to whatever might emerge from their efforts. While they didn't fully know what the outcomes might be, they were committed to their aspiration of a better, more authentic, and more engaging learning experience for every student.

Once they had the first iteration or prototype, they worked from there in a process of appreciative inquiry, looking for more equitable opportunities for each student and identifying strategies that seemed effective. That meant talking to all stakeholders, including teachers, students, parents, and the broader community, to look at the project's success through multiple lenses. Andy explains: "We could look at this project and the impact it had for students. Students' voices were heard. Whether they were in gifted or special education or spoke another language, they all wanted to do the project and to do their best work because they knew they were going to be heard."

CO-ENACTING A BETTER FUTURE AT ATTUCKS MIDDLE SCHOOL

As we described in Chapter 7, Deirdre Williams started her principalship at Attucks Middle School by working on culture and relationships among students, adults, and the community. That came first. Next, she and the leadership team turned their attention to looking at work products produced by both students and teachers. They believed that looking at student work together would help them better understand the work students were asked to do, whether it reflected high expectations, and if it would truly prepare students for high school and beyond. "We started trying to understand where we were teaching. Were we teaching too low? We got to conversations where teachers started owning, 'I need help with this.'"

Teachers and administrators at Attucks were ready to make the turn toward cocreating the future, to learn together how to hold high expectations for students. One of the first aspirational questions they considered was "What if every student attained a high school credit in middle school?" That meant providing support to both students and their teachers. Deirdre knew the school would not only have to believe it, but make that belief and learning public. As they turned toward an unknown future, she "always wanted teachers to feel supported." One way she sought to provide support was to create a full-time position for a professional learning community facilitator. With skillful and consistent planning and facilitation, these small groups became forums for teachers to open up about their work and engage in cycles of feedback and improvement as they posed and responded to increasingly challenging questions.

As the school co-enacted the future, how teachers and leaders interacted and collaborated changed and was reinvented. Rather than school leaders telling the teachers what to do, teachers and leaders discussed issues such as classroom management together. Experienced teachers became a source of knowledge and skill in these discussions, building on what was working (appreciative inquiry) and prototyping classroom management approaches (improvement science). "We would act approaches out. First-year teachers talked through scenarios with our experienced teachers. Everyone created a classroom culture action plan to describe what they were going to implement and what support they needed and shared it for feedback." Teachers and leaders collaboratively co-enacted the discussed scenario responses in their classrooms and across the school and continued to refine their understanding and practice, shaping a new school culture and working toward a better future.

ANDRES LOPEZ'S STORY 12: CO-ENACTING

Andres shares how he built an action space in his setting.

I build support for the class so that many people feel they are part of the reason why the class exists and continues. Because then you have a lot of people with you protecting and promoting the class. Strategically, I crowd-sourced to get the money for the books. I knew that I could ask friends for money to order the books, but I wanted it to be a public opportunity to tell people, "Hey, this class exists. It's the first of its kind." It's a chance to get people to think, "I want to be a part of whatever is occurring there."

CO-ENACTING AN ASPIRATIONAL FUTURE

In the enacting phase of the deep dive, the leader's attention is on an aspirational or "what if" future—the reason why the dive was made in the first place. Leaders need to ensure that the future is cocreated and co-enacted so that ownership and responsibility are shared. As leaders and their colleagues move through the "what if" work, five tactics are helpful: (1) authorizing "what if" thinking and actions, (2) widening the circle of leadership, (3) practicing co-enacting in public, (4) creating opportunities to listen, and (5) managing momentum. These tactics represent a departure from the Common Theory approach to school improvement. They enlarge possible responses rather than narrow them, support collaboration, promote ownership, and share responsibility.

Tactic 1: Authorizing "What If" Thinking and Actions

Focusing on strengths and imagining "what if" characterized the anticipatory mindset adopted by Andy and Deirdre. Moving toward an unknown future with confidence requires Andy's moon-shot thinking. "You aren't just trying to think about the next step you are going to take, but thinking ten times beyond, where you shoot for the moon and see where you really end up landing."

Likewise, Deirdre, in spite of being a 1st-year principal in what was considered a "failing school," kept imagining "what if." She recalls,

> I used to say they had no business putting a 1st-year principal here. Now I retract that because I realize that I couldn't see anything but the possibility of success, and that is what we aimed toward. Had I been an experienced principal, when some things didn't go well, I might have second-guessed myself. But as it was, I went in saying "we can do this" and we kept at it until we did.

It was this "what if" approach that propelled Deirdre and Andy out of the turn of the dive and into enacting an emerging future. Maintaining confidence and focusing on strengths requires leaders not to react or intervene into what is, but to build an action space for cocreating the future (Chapter 6). This shift requires focusing their intention, attention, and listening for what could come to be (Scharmer, 2018). Andy and Deirdre built that kind of space in their respective settings by initially envisioning it and sharing that vision with others. Scharmer (2018) writes that when leaders open their ideas to not only the universe of their organizations but also beyond, the universe will bring suggestions and opportunities. The challenge then becomes to make "your own calculations about which ones are helpful" (p. 119).

Deirdre and Andy built on and continued to cultivate relationships and capacity formed in the observing and turning phases of the dive, as they embarked with their colleagues and students on a series of experiments and prototypes. For Andy, that often meant working with one teacher from a team who was ready to take risks. The resulting prototype then served as a joining-in point for those teachers who previously could not imagine the new vision in action without an example; they were able to contribute to the next iteration that became more widely coconstructed.

The "what if" goal at Attucks Middle School included creating high school credit courses to demonstrate high expectations and a clearer path to high school success. Slow and steady efforts meant Deirdre could tell the community that "by the end of year 3, we had seven courses for high school credit."

Tactic 2: Widening the Circle of Leadership

In this chapter and previous ones, we highlight the deeply personal commitment that leaders make to schools and students. It is this commitment that initially compels them to undertake a deep dive. As leaders and their organizations move through the phases of the dive, this focus on personal commitment shifts to the group. To be successful, leaders and their colleagues must move from an individual commitment to a shared, relational responsibility. There is no other way.

A deep dive challenges all educators to be learners. Moving through the phases of the dive individually and collectively, beliefs and assumptions change to become more equitable, true, and reflective to guide action and cocreate the future. This is transformational learning (Mezirow, 2000).

Enacting in practice must necessarily be co-enacting, which makes different demands on leadership than observing or turning. Authorizing "what if" thinking means authorizing others to embrace aspirational thinking and to take action toward it, supporting them as they do. Leaders create a safe space for the community to engage in "what if" thinking, and trust that during the earlier phases of observing and turning enough capacity was built for the school to be successful in co-enacting. Ultimately, co-enacting requires shared practice that makes visible that all are learning by doing, the leader included.

During this enacting phase of the dive, Andy and Deirdre used a variety of tools, strategies, and platforms to share prototypes that were being tried out and refined. They used social media, professional organizations and partners, and learning communities to share and gather feedback. Similar to the other leaders in this book, Andy and Deirdre were highly visible models of the values and assumptions about teaching and learning that they espoused. For example, Deirdre used these values as criteria for recruitment. And both Deirdre and Andy used them to determine how they utilized resources, whether it was hiring a full-time person to facilitate learning communities at Attucks or dedicating a budget for a student-led book selection committee at Barrow.

By visibly engaging in the same behaviors they were asking of others—risk taking, public sharing of work, seeking feedback, using espoused values as a lens for decisionmaking—Deirdre and Andy were co-learning and copracticing in public alongside their colleagues and students. These actions enriched collective capacity, shared ownership and accountability, and widened leadership. They trusted and embraced the wisdom and ingenuity of their colleagues and students. They were no longer the sole owners of the future, rather they were cocreating and co-enacting it as it emerged. For example, when Attucks started videoing teachers leading lessons in their classrooms, Deirdre was also videoed leading faculty learning experiences. Videos were jointly analyzed for strengths and improvements.

At Barrow Elementary School, Andy asked colleagues to make their lesson plans, student work, and instruction public to others in the school and beyond on social media. He always went first, sharing his thinking and planning with a broad audience on his blog and Twitter account. He sought feedback through regular interactions with other library media and technology specialists and his across-school learning community. Their actions are reminiscent of what Safir (2018) reminds us when she writes about cocreating an emerging future:

> Emergence suggests an uncomfortable truth: As a leader, you may be in charge, but you're not in control. If we are used to holding the reins of power tightly, this approach requires a mindset shift; we must believe in the ability of teacher leaders to solve our toughest challenges. Coupled with an investment in time and training, this shift allows for innovative

solutions to emerge at the grassroots level and energize a school culture. For the process to work, principals must articulate a vision and direction, trust in teachers to take real leadership, and then be quiet enough to notice and amplify promising ideas. (pp. 70–71)

For Andy and Deirdre, this meant they had to articulate a vision and direction, and they had to believe in the ability of colleagues to join them in co-enacting a better future on behalf of their students and communities.

Tactic 3: Co-Enacting in Public

It is significant that at both Barrow and Attucks all the educators involved made their learning public, to one another and to audiences beyond the school. By disrupting individual, privatized practice and making learning public, the future opened to new possibilities. These practices of opening up private practice to shared inquiry (appreciative inquiry) and learning-by-doing (improvement science) in public begin in the observing phase of the dive and persist as educators move into the enacting phase. It is through these cycles of public learning and feedback that prototypes are refined and culture is shaped and enacted.

Andy initially made his work public by posting his ideas and questions on his blog, which got the attention of his principal. The principal then created opportunities for Andy to make his ideas public within his school community, and she put in place structures for him to work with the teachers at his school in planning meetings.

The mission and goals Andy created for the library media center explicitly stated values about learning. He shared them widely and attracted colleagues who wanted to join him. The public nature of these statements also served to hold the group accountable as they created prototypes and experimented with ways to realize them. Furthermore, going public helped Andy find like-minded collaborators across the United States and globally.

During the Barrow Peace Prize project, Andy reached out to educational technology companies for technical expertise. One company, Capstone, asked if they could talk with students about their product and how it could be improved. A media site, FlipGrid, participated in the awards ceremony virtually and featured it on its website. This reach beyond the school turned a school-based prototype into an internationally recognized phenomenon. As a result, students were not only cocreators and co-inventors in a school project but also in the development of an educational technology.

ANDRES LOPEZ'S STORY 13: CO-ENACTING

Students and community donors also shaped Andres's prototypes.

The first time I taught the class, the students would ask if they could keep the books we were reading. What English teacher wants to tell a kid they can't keep a book? I doubled down on the crowdsourcing approach, because there's no way a school is going to buy a set of books to give away to kids every year. I asked the community if they were comfortable with me asking for books every year so that students could keep the books and [the community] stepped up.

Tactic 4: Deliberately Creating Opportunities to Listen

For Andy and his colleagues, the most important voices became those of Barrow students and their families. They were the reason for the turn. The students and the larger community could tell him and his colleagues how they were doing in reinventing students' learning experiences.

Students were asked for project feedback through multiple avenues, and they were listened to. One idea that emerged from students was the creation of an actual trophy instead of the paper award previously used. The next year's Peace Prize featured trophies designed and created by students on the media center's 3-D printers, in collaboration with the art teacher. Now the student-designed prize is awarded annually. Barrow students cocreated alongside their teachers, and together they moved through the co-enacting phase of the deep dive, realizing and shaping an emerging culture that embodied the practices and attitude of moon-shot thinking.

Through Andy's blog and media center website, the Peace Prize project was shared as it evolved. This included live-streaming the awards ceremony. While this added more complexity and public exposure, Andy learned that watching the ceremony was especially well-received by families who could not be there in person. This public sharing expanded engagement and responses from families. It "provided an opportunity for parents or family members to see their child's work in a way they hadn't been able to see it before." It also offered a platform for families to share their responses, questions, and concerns with Andy and his colleagues.

At Attucks, the formation of small learning communities was one tool the school community used to open their previously private work to a wider audience. They also made extensive use of video as a tool for learning and making practice public as well. Deirdre shares,

We weren't just going to video the teachers teaching, we videoed
leaders giving feedback to teachers, and I was videoed giving
coaching feedback to my leaders. I was in the mix. It wasn't one of
those things where we are going to do this for teachers, but we don't
have to do it. You need to be an instructional leader first, which
meant your "classroom" was fair game and you should be able to
deliver a lesson.

Deirdre and the school leaders created deliberate opportunities to receive feedback and listen. And, of course, school data and student learning data were made public. Every time they looked at data, they would do
it together posing probing questions (Thompson-Grove, 2018b). Deirdre
notes that the school became really good at asking probing questions. At
first, the leaders would look at the data ahead of time and frame probing
questions. Soon teachers were taking that on. They were asking questions
like "What do we need to do?" and "What can we do differently?"

Within their learning communities, the teachers began using protocols or agreed-upon structures to delve more deeply and reflectively into
student-generated and teacher-generated work such as assessments, lesson plans, and projects (see Chapter 4). They were looking for evidence of
impact and, through their work together, learning to develop and analyze
dependable evidence for continued inquiry (Donohoo et al., 2018). Deirdre was able to listen to the questions teachers were generating and to the
conversations that were ensuing.

Both Deirdre and Andy and their colleagues created deliberate opportunities to listen to others. Listening is an essential part of improvement
science and appreciative inquiry processes. Hearing from others provides a
chance to learn about and reflect on the success and shortfalls of a prototype from multiple points of view. The new insight and information help
pinpoint how a prototype might be refined and improved as it evolves.
Leaders have to be "quiet enough to notice and amplify promising ideas"
(Safir, 2018, p. 71). Deliberately creating listening opportunities is essential.

Tactic 5: Managing Momentum

Coming out of the turn, energized by conviction and purpose, focused
on a better future, and ready to enact experiments and prototypes to see
how they will land, leaders find that there is momentum to manage. At
this stage of the deep dive a new culture is being shaped. The organization
has existing internal and external capacity to use, and anxiety is being
harnessed as energy and impetus for forward movement (see also Table
7.1) Leaders and organizations now have to manage momentum so that
culture can solidify and crystallize (Scharmer, 2018). Capacity needs to be

---

ANDRES LOPEZ'S STORY 14: CO-ENACTING

Andres knew he was "going in the right direction" when momentum and collective capacity began to build.

Teachers started coming to me asking, "What books could I incorporate in my American Literature class?" That's a big part of my why [purpose], to spread the possibility. Now I'm duplicating my classroom library, so that it's more available to teachers and I can say "I'm going to email you with different ways that I use these books." I want to be in a position to do that.

---

carefully expended, and anxiety kept low enough, to allow the inquiry initiatives to fully cycle through and be learned from. It's not just doing, but learning by doing. Andy describes how momentum built at his school after the Barrow Peace Prize project:

> Now they are always saying, what else can we do this year? And sometimes I have to remind them that some of these things happen because of taking risks and showing the work. The more I have taken a risk and seen big things happen, or even small things, things I didn't plan to have happen, helps me be better at taking a risk. But everyone's not in the same place as me, and I have to take into consideration where each teacher—and student—is on their journey.

When the focus is on enacting, it would be tempting to want to pick up the pace. It is also tempting for front-runners to push the pace, or for those outside of the organization with some attached accountability (e.g., district offices, funders) to push for more, faster. Undertaking the creative and risky work of a deep dive in this era of federal, state, and local mandates and testing requirements also affects momentum.

In high-need schools such as Deirdre's, the threat of school closure loomed. Deirdre carefully kept the long view in mind, working with patient urgency and looking for important points of cultural inculcation to assess how far the school had come and where together they could go. "There was still so much room to grow, and yet I knew we were going in the right direction when we had students who received special education services and English language learners in high school credit courses." Deirdre and Andy watched for signs of momentum, and also knew it had to be carefully managed.

Importantly, Andy and Deirdre's work in their schools took place over years. It takes time to build the relational trust that each developed with their colleagues and communities. Learning together takes time, and this is where processes such as discussion-based protocols can be helpful in order to both slow down and move along. Protocols, as described in Chapters 3 and 4, provide intentionality and efficiency in conversational and group process and pace.

Just as all the leaders in the previous chapters, Andy and Deirdre continued to observe, listen, reflect, and learn alongside their colleagues and students as they collectively engaged in various experiments and prototypes. They didn't get stuck in analyzing and talking about what happened but kept moving to the next step toward the future. This tenacious attention and intention are essential at every phase of the dive.

THE GOOD NEWS ABOUT THIS HARD WORK: CREATING ENDURING CAPACITY

The good news is that building and enacting the collective capacity that takes place in this phase and in earlier ones creates enduring future capacity (refer to Figure 2.5 in Chapter 2 for a visual that depicts this). Civic or political will or resources might diminish or disappear, but collective capacity persists. Once group members successfully build and use their collective capacity, it becomes easier to do the next time. The bonds created within the group tend to be permanent, even when members change (Scharmer, 2009).

In Chapters 7 and 8, we have described the third and final phase of the deep dive, enacting and co-enacting. After the hard and risky work of observing, turning, and enacting, leaders and schools emerge from the dive with a greater sense of agency; a more critical understanding of the assumptions underlying their individual and collective values, beliefs, and practices; processes to take better actions and make more informed and reflective decisions; and aspiration for a more dependable, robust, and equitable future.

CHAPTER 9

A Book for Activists

Our challenge, and calling, as educators is to find faith in humanity, in the everyday, and in our interactions with youth. We must seek to find something to give us hope in every student that we see.

—Andres Lopez

This is a book for activists. It is a book for educators who are committed to and have a sense of urgency around deep change and the reinvention of schools. These educators take up the most difficult questions about the purpose of schools, the meaning of teaching and learning, and equitable educational practice. However, the argument of the preceding eight chapters is that a "deep commitment" about this work is a necessary, but by no means sufficient, component of the work of activists. Adding commitment and urgency to the Common Theory gets schools to the same superficial place, except with added pressure and new rhetoric. Commitment and urgency turn up the heat on the Common Theory, but the results are often the same. Figure 9.1 captures this version of the Common Theory.

Turning up the heat on the Common Theory still ignores the competing commitments, hidden rules, deeply held beliefs, and longstanding traditions that characterize schools. Turning up the heat ignores the deep currents, ancient muck, and sunken wrecks at the bottom of the harbor of school improvement. Schein (2016) calls the act of turning up the heat "increasing survival anxiety" (p. 322). Survival anxiety asks educators to relinquish their existing professional self and replace it with an untested and unfamiliar identity.

Turning up the heat, or increasing "survival anxiety" alone, is unlikely to lead to deep change. Schein writes that "From the change leader's point of view, it might seem obvious that the way to motivate learning is simply to increase the survival anxiety or guilt. The problem with that approach is that greater threat or guilt may simply increase defensiveness to avoid the threat or pain of the learning process" (p. 327). Simply increasing pressure or urgency does not by itself lead to the reinvention of schools. Something different is needed.

Figure 9.1. Turning Up the Heat on the Common Theory

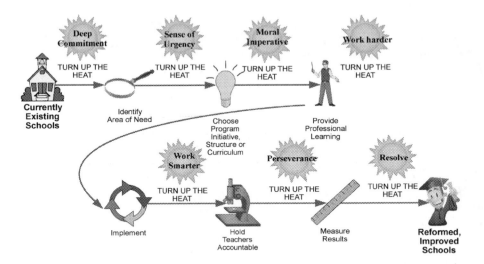

BEYOND TURNING UP THE HEAT

That "something different" is the deep dive, an UnCommon Theory that is complicated, risky, and calls upon educators to understand adult development, school culture, and organizational change theory. It asks leaders like Jed Lippard to "lead with developmental intent," and to see clearly "what this place needs" as Liz Ozuna tells us. A deep dive asks school leaders to "be persistently nagged" by inequitable practice, as Matt Underwood was, and "to help everyone to become human," as Deirdre Williams aspired to. A deep dive is not a prepackaged program. It is not a recipe with numerated steps and predictable outcomes. A deep dive asks a lot. And the deeper the dive, the more it asks, both of the leader and the school community.

The deep dive is challenging because it is full of persistent pressures, unsettled paradoxes, and unresolved tensions that leaders need to carefully navigate and make sense of. Rather than using the more academic language of "paradoxes" and "tensions" to describe the challenges of the deep dive, we have chosen to look at these challenges from a leader's perspective.

CONTRADICTORY ADVICE ON NAVIGATING THE DEEP DIVE

The deep dive asks leaders to confront and live with a variety of contradictory advice. For example, the deep dive asks leaders to work with others, as Matt Underwood recommends when he says that "the learning is tough, but we will do it together." At the same time, leaders often must work alone. Cathy O'Connell realized that she "needed to take control and put it out there." Thus the deep dive asks leaders to work collaboratively *and* to lead, to be the first to "walk out on thin air" (Liz Ozuna). The advice seems complicated and even contradictory, but effective leaders cannot avoid the tensions of the deep dive. They cannot resolve them. They have to live with, manage, and make sense of them.

One of the ways leaders manage the contradictory advice of the deep dive is by "reframing" (McDonald, 2014, p. 5; McDonald et al., 2018). A frame is when "we ordinarily see what we expect to see and also what we like to see" (p. 5). Frames are made up of fundamental assumptions—assumptions that exist mainly out of sight, at the bottom of the harbor of school improvement. When leaders reframe contradictory advice, they offer the school community new ways of thinking about deeply held beliefs and downloaded patterns of the past. To reinvent schools, leaders must help their schools to reframe.

In our view, there are at least four pieces of contradictory advice that leaders need to make sense of in order to navigate the deep dive:

1. Understand that observing is more important than doing, *and* doing is more important than observing.
2. Work collaboratively within a group, *and* be prepared to lead.
3. Work on culture persistently and intentionally, *and* do not work on culture directly.
4. Recognize that adult learning is limited by adult development, *and* adult development is limited by adult learning.

Contradictory Advice 1: Observing is more important than doing, *and* doing is more important than observing.

Scharmer (2009) contends that organizations are powerfully held by "patterns of the past" (p. 39), by the ways that they have always done things. Schein (2016) calls these patterns "fundamental assumptions," which hold us even more than we hold them. McDonald (2014) calls them "frames." These patterns of the past, fundamental assumptions, or frames lie at the very bottom of the harbor of school improvement, buried in decades of muck, and consequently are almost completely invisible to us.

When schools use tools such as the protocols described in Chapter 4, they learn to observe themselves and their invisible practices, and they often uncover anxiety-producing revelations. For example, when Liz began to help her school observe their patterns of the past, they learned that "a fear was that we could not change the culture of our school and our small town to expect kids would be successful." Similarly, at Attucks Middle School, Deirdre helped the community see their frame that "Attucks was a place to house those students who were not going to get in somewhere else." Helping the community learn to see their invisible practices and assumptions is long-term, difficult work because these submerged assumptions and practices are often at odds with the school's espoused values (high expectations for all, rigorous curriculum, and so on).

Seeing is more important than doing because learning to see, and becoming comfortable with what is uncovered, is so difficult that the reinvention of deep practices is impossible unless schools can learn to see. However, the goal of the deep dive is not only to learn to see, but also to work toward the reinvention of schools. *Seeing* can be so difficult that it might seem like an end in and of itself. It is not.

Cathy O'Connell and Michael Maloney spent a year in the North Reading Middle School 2.0 project helping the school learn to see even the most difficult aspects of their practice. The school learned to see how "students weren't given an equal opportunity to learn at a high level." This is a difficult and anxiety-producing revelation, and the school could have easily stopped its work right there. But Cathy knew that the ultimate goal was *doing*, not *observing*. "I think also we were probably maybe a little afraid, but at some point you've got to grab hold and say 'This is what we're going to do.'" It was in the turn that the school transitioned from seeing to doing, and it was the principal who ensured that the transition happened.

Reframing, holding, and using the contradictory advice depends on a mental shift that goes beyond understanding the phases of the deep dive. The first phase of the dive is observing, and without that capacity there is no deep dive, no surfacing of fundamental assumptions, and no wondering about the patterns of the past. However, for the dive to lead to deep change and the reinvention of schools, observing needs to eventually turn to doing, and enacting an emerging future.

The reframe required of leaders is that seeing and doing are reciprocal; they are connected, two sides of the same coin, and they are both essential for the deep dive—however, not at the same time. UnCommon leaders understand that if *observing* is hard and a group feels stuck, then it might be time to turn to *doing*. Similarly, if the *doing* is unproductive and strained, then the school might need to *observe* more. All of our leaders toggled between seeing and doing, doing and seeing, diving deeper each time the school made a transition. Each movement in the dive leads to what Deb Holman called "a deep dive into some stuff that is tougher, and really about adults." The work is cyclical, ongoing, reciprocal, and enduring.

Contradictory Advice 2: Work collaboratively, *and* be prepared to lead.

Every leader we interviewed explained that the deep dive is a collaborative effort. Matt, for example, engaged his community in conversations about the mission of the school, helped the faculty collect and analyze demographic data and student work, and organized a State of the School meeting during the observing phase. Moreover, he regularly used texts about race, class, and equitable educational practice to inform many faculty and community meetings. Enacting a deep dive is a community-wide enterprise; no leader wants to arrive at the end of the dive alone, without enacting deep change.

Further, the leaders all adopted very intentional strategies to avoid leading alone. Matt put it this way: "I also know that getting out of this bubble in which I work is really important." Our leaders had coaches, mentors, and networks of like-minded educators. They brought in outside facilitators, engaged in collaborative inquiry projects, and presented at conferences. They made every effort, on every level, to not work alone. Yet they also had to lead. They had to step beyond the safety of the group and even stand in momentary opposition. They had to be the first to turn, to step into the uncertain and emerging future.

The leaders in this book did this in two ways. First, they all held unique roles in the deep dive. Jed was the "chief dot connector." Liz was "the original sense maker." Andy was the "moon-shot thinker," and Deirdre was the "'what if?' asker." Each of our leaders adopted a unique stance in the work of the deep dive. It was a stance that only the leader could take, and without it there could be no deep dive. Each leader had a unique responsibility and was often the first to step into the emerging future.

The leaders also were prepared to lead during the times that the dive produced the most anxiety, especially at the turn. Jed explains: "I think that means making some decisions about what is going to be our priority." A deep dive does not happen easily or by chance. Leaders sometimes need to make decisions about priorities, especially when the dive is beginning to uncover uncomfortable truths such as "students weren't given an equal opportunity to learn at a high level" (Cathy), or "Attucks was a place to house those students who were not going to get in somewhere else" (Deirdre). The anxiety produced by seeing uncomfortable truths has to be held (Heifetz & Linsky, 2004), and the leader has to hold it.

Reframing, holding, and using the contradictory advice is contingent on understanding that leaders' work in the deep dive is multifaceted. In most phases of the deep dive, leaders need to be as collaborative and inclusive as possible. A deep dive is a collaborative venture that leads to co-enacting the future. Jed recounted: "Initially, common planning time was a core requirement and professional expectation; then, creating the structures inside of that time and space ensured that meaningful work is actually happening, which then evolved into collaborative inquiry." Leaders don't work alone because the work cannot be done alone.

However, leaders also hold unique responsibilities for the success of a deep dive. Leaders assess when the school is ready for a deep dive, how deep the dive might be, and how to hold and manage anxiety at critical junctures. Andy, for example, held a unique vision around "giving students, teachers, and families opportunities to dream, tinker, create, and share." Deirdre similarly recounts, "I saw another picture for the kids in that community. I went with the picture I saw." At the beginning Deirdre and Andy—and no one else—held the vision.

The reframe required to hold and live with this contradictory advice is understanding the unique responsibilities and roles that leaders hold in a deep dive, and how those responsibilities and roles vary depending on dive timing and phase. In the observing part of the dive, a leader works collaboratively, but at times, especially as a school learns to observe, the leader also needs to lead alone in order to structure and support the school's learning. The leader's responsibility in this phase is to support the school community as it examines its closely held practices and traditions, deep assumptions, and fundamental values. During the turning part of the dive, the leader holds the anxiety that the observing phase generates, and moves the school from seeing to enacting. In the turn, the leader needs to hold the school's anxiety and be the first to "walk out on thin air."

The essential ingredient is timing. If the leader spends too much time in the observing phase of the dive, it stalls. Yet, if the leader moves too quickly to enacting, the community might not be able to tolerate the anxiety generated by the turn. In every case, it is the leader's responsibility to think about process and timing.

Contradictory Advice 3: Work on culture persistently and intentionally *and* not directly.

Right from the very beginning, this book has been about organizational culture. We relied on Schein's (2016) framework to highlight levels of culture. We argued that the deeper the dive, the more fundamental assumptions will be disturbed, the more anxiety will be released, and the more possibilities to reinvent schools will surface. We conceptualize this idea in Figure 9.2.

Moreover, our school leaders seemed well aware of the importance of organizational culture. Cathy O'Connell explained that "when you

Figure 9.2. Reviewing Culture, Anxiety, and Change and the Deep Dive

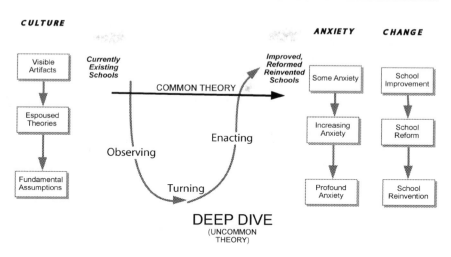

DEEP DIVE
(UNCOMMON
THEORY)

change something like leveling in a school that's always leveled, that's a real deep dive into fundamental stuff with the school. It doesn't get too much more fundamental than that." Culture is about the "fundamental stuff" that the school is built on. However, as Matt Underwood suggests, disturbing the fundamental stuff is challenging and easily avoided. "You have all these challenges, and dealing with something that has to do with class and race quickly falls down people's priority list." Each of our leaders discussed, often at great length, the power of "unconscious, taken-for-granted beliefs and values" (Schein, 2016, p. 17). Yet none of them had an improvement plan designed to work directly on organizational culture. They did, however, have a clear strategy for working indirectly, but very intentionally, on organizational culture.

School leaders who try to directly change or improve the culture of a school often conflate school *culture* and *climate*. They organize staff breakfasts, dress-down Fridays, team building exercises, and end-of-year parties. These strategies exist at the level of visible artifacts or espoused values, and are designed to create school *climates,* where people get along and like each other, not school *cultures,* where educators grapple with the thorniest issues of school reinvention and manage the anxiety that those issues surface.

Modifying school culture requires a change in the hidden patterns, assumptions, and long-held values of the community. However, this cannot be done in the same way that schools buy textbooks, implement a new science program, or build a new schedule. Because culture, to a large degree, holds us and is consequently mostly invisible, it can only be changed indirectly and slowly. It has to be learned and taught.

An example of indirectly teaching culture is the use of discussion-based protocols (see Chapter 4). At Mathis, Liz began her work by having the faculty examine texts connected to the new work. She did not announce that she was directly working on school culture, yet she also understood that having a common intellectual experience would disturb some of the isolationism, conservatism, and presentism (Hargreaves & Shirley, 2009; Lortie, 1975) that characterized the school. Liz intentionally disturbed patterns of interactions and assumptions, but she never directly declared that she was working on school culture when she used text-based protocols to scaffold difficult conversations.

These conversations were designed to help faculty become accustomed to the discomfort of having an opinion that differs from a colleague's. Eventually, Liz added reflective questions about both process and content to help faculty find new ways of being with one another. She never worked directly on school culture. It was never part of a strategic plan. She helped the school *be* the new culture. She was *always* working on school culture.

Reframing, holding, and using the contradictory advice requires recognizing that school culture is taught and learned. It cannot be found on a website or implemented like new state standards. School culture is learned over time and taught to members of the community by each other. The Common Theory approach is of little value for this sort of learning.

Learning a different school culture, like all complicated learning, involves exposing and questioning familiar patterns, and painstakingly learning the new practices, assumptions, and values that will replace them. In this pedagogy, discovering, co-creating, and questioning are more important—and useful—than direct instruction.

The reframe needed to manage this contradictory advice is to remember that leaders have both spoken and unspoken learning agendas. The spoken—*and* shared *and* published—agenda is connected to the phases of the deep dive. The spoken agenda details the learning the group will undertake, texts the group will consider, protocols that will be used to examine practice, and ideas the group will prototype. The unspoken agenda—carried quietly, mostly by the leader—is about indirectly learning new ways of being together. The unspoken agenda is the thinking behind asking teachers to share their practice, consider new ideas, work in more collaborative ways, and dig into their norms and values. The unspoken agenda is the leader's way of working indirectly, but intentionally and persistently, on school culture.

Contradictory Advice 4: Adult learning is limited by adult development, *and* adult development is limited by adult learning.

Schools are places where adults learn. Educators are asked to learn new curricula, new reading strategies, new ways to use time, and new teaching practices. Every stage of a deep dive depends on adult learning. At Prospect Hill Academy, Jed helped teachers learn the skills of collaborative inquiry. At Mathis, teachers learned about global studies (Asia Society, 2018). At Barrow Elementary, teachers learned a new way of thinking about their students' ability to direct their own learning.

Adult learning is particularly important in the enactment phase of the deep dive. For example at Attucks, teachers used an appreciative inquiry approach to enact structures that recognized teachers whose students were doing well, who regularly shared their work, and who collaboratively developed model lessons. At Barrow, teachers learned an approach to teaching and learning in which students were the drivers of their own learning. They used the Barrow Peace Prize concept to pilot this new approach to teaching and learning. Enacting is about adult learning. The deep dive is about adult learning.

However, the deep dive also depends on adult development (see Chapter 3). At Prospect Hill Academy, Jed described how, as "chief adult developer, [I] was trying to lead from a place of developmental intention." On the simplest level this meant, "having some knowledge of the fact that adults make meaning in qualitatively different ways." Jed understood, for example, that instrumental knowers required one type of feedback, while socializing knowers responded better with a different type of feedback.

Yet leading with developmental intent entails more than simply understanding and being strategic about the different ways that adults in schools make meaning. Adult development impacts *what* adults learn and *how* they learn it. For example, at Mathis, Liz quickly ran up against "the Mathis way," the deeply held pattern of traditions and assumptions that defined "how we do things around here." Liz understood that the community could never enact the new future of an ISSN school unless it could learn to think in more complicated ways, consider a variety of perspectives, and, most important, understand that "the Mathis way" was only one way of doing things. Liz needed to engage in adult development work because the school community was limited in the learning it was capable of.

Liz started adult development work slowly. She engaged the community in conversations about their hopes and fears around the Mathis way, and she used texts and protocols to expand the faculty's capacity to think more broadly and stay in difficult conversations. Eventually the school community developed the capacity to examine, understand, and rethink their assumptions about their expectations for their students.

Without adult development work—without helping the community become more complex thinkers, more able to stay in uncomfortable conversations, and more willing to consider a variety of perspectives on the most challenging issues—Liz's dive would have been short and shallow.

Every one of our leaders engaged in adult development work. Cathy used the NRMS 2.0 structure to build capacity. Matt used faculty meetings and community time to practice talking about issues of race and equity. Deirdre and Jed helped their schools take a collaborative inquiry approach to improving their practice. Andres persistently raised troubling questions about the ways the school served Latino students. The reason that the leaders invested so much time and effort in adult development work is that, unless school communities have the capacity to work collaboratively, give each other useful feedback, make their practice public, stay in difficult conversations, and think in complicated ways, then the school will never successfully address the deepest issues of race, equity, and reinvention. The deeper the dive, the more is demanded of the adults who undertake it.

The deeper a dive goes, the more it disturbs fundamental assumptions—like the "Mathis way"—and the more anxiety it surfaces; the deeper the change, the more adult development is required. To a great degree, adult development determines the depth of any dive (see Figure 5.2). A school that is primarily instrumental, that can only follow the "Mathis way," can only undertake a shallow dive. The reason our leaders spent so much time on adult development work is that they understood that the deepest dives—addressing low expectations for students at Mathis, or inequitable group practices at North Reading Middle School, or unbalanced admissions practice at Atlanta Neighborhood Charter School, or pushing Latino students out of school in San Antonio—require adult and school communities who are comfortable with disagreement, are resistant to easy answers, have the courage to speak their own truths, and are able to surface and explore their own assumptions.

The demands of adult development on school communities apply equally to school leadership. Instrumental knowers are comfortable leading the Common Theory. Following a recipe with clear concrete steps is precisely what instrumental knowers—and leaders—want. However, deeper dives demand more of school communities and of school leaders. In our view, the deepest dives into issues of race, equity, and school reinvention, where the future is not entirely known, require self-authoring or self-transforming leaders. Our leaders understood that they were leading their schools into futures that were largely unknown but had to be enacted because of their commitment to a fair and equitable future.

The deep dive was propelled by adult development, and the leaders understood that for the work to be successful they needed to welcome negative opinions, sit with unanswered questions, hold the school's and their own anxiety, and have the courage to speak their own truth as the dive unfolded.

Reframing, holding, and using the contradictory advice is contingent on being clear about the question, "What do the adults in the school community need *now*?" If the adults need to learn the latest procedure for getting kids on a bus at the end of the day, then adult learning is more important than adult development. However, if adults need to learn new and yet-unimagined practices that address the complex needs of each and every child, and end the predictive value attached to qualities such as race, language, sexual identity, and cognitive profile, then adult development work is essential. Adult development determines what can be learned and how it will be learned.

The reframe that this contradictory advice necessitates is connected to the reciprocal nature of adult learning and adult development. Adults in all schools are asked to learn. However, the depth and breadth of that learning varies widely. Some schools struggle with adopting a new textbook, while others have learned to dig deeply into complicated performance data, while still others want to learn more about the assumptions and practices that limit the learning of some of their students. In each case, the adults are learning what they are *ready* to learn. The instrumental knowers are learning concrete steps and the socializing knowers are wondering about group practice. In every case adult learning is both fostered and limited by adult development.

However, to achieve the reinvention of schools, the wondering, examining, and surfacing of complicated thinking associated with adult development work has to turn into adult learning, into a structure to try out, a prototype to test, an initiative to launch, or a model to implement. In general, if adult learning seems stalled, then adult development work is needed; conversely, if adult development work seems too difficult, then adult learning is required. UnCommon leaders ask and understand what a school and its community need to learn *now*.

REMINDERS ABOUT CONTRADICTORY ADVICE AND REFRAMING

Reframing contradictory advice is not easy, but it is essential. One challenge is that leaders receive so much contradictory advice. In the discussion above, we unpacked four of the most complicated pieces of contradictory advice that leaders need to reframe. Yet there are many more. A few examples are:

- A leader is just a steward of the deep dive, it's not personal, *and* as the leader, it is always "your" deep dive, it's always personal
- A leader can expect to have to "push" others in a deep dive, *and* a leader needs to allow being pushed by others
- A leader needs to expect and accept resistance on all fronts, *and* a leader can be the greatest obstacle
- A leader in a deep dive needs to be confident, *and* a leader needs to be vulnerable

Given these and countless other paradoxes inherent in the deep dive process, leaders must focus on two essential leadership tasks. The first is simply to expect, accept, and even embrace the idea that the deep dive is full of tensions, paradoxes, and contradictory advice. The more that this is understood and accepted, the more that leaders can help their communities navigate the tensions inherent in the deep dive. There is no other way. This is not the Common Theory. There is no recipe.

The second essential leadership task is reframing, making sense of the contradictions and tensions. Every one of our leaders modeled this essential task as "chief dot connectors," "moon-shot thinkers," or "original sense makers." Leadership in the deep dive not only embraces the contradictions and tensions of the dive, but also reframes and makes sense of them for the community. While not every piece of contradictory advice will be deftly reframed, UnCommon leaders get better and better at seeing, naming, and helping their communities live with these tensions.

Expecting and accepting contradictions, and the ability to make sense of them, are not just the two essential leadership tasks of the deep dive; they are also characteristics of the self-transforming stage of adult development. Self-transforming knowers are suspicious of absolutes and consequently comfortable with ambiguity and contradictory advice (Kegan, 1998). Furthermore, self-transforming knowers—unlike instrumental, socializing, and even self-authoring knowers—embrace conflict as a means to find more complete, justified, and useful reframes. For self-transforming knowers, framing and reframing and reframing again are vital parts of the deepest dives that lead to school reinvention. Each dive creates more tension, releases more anxiety, and at the same time creates more meaning, more capacity, and more possibility.

The implication is quite straightforward. The hardest adult development work that leaders do is with themselves. If the leader cannot embrace conflict, the school cannot. If the leader cannot tolerate ambiguity, the school will not. If the leader cannot reframe contradiction, then the school cannot. If the leader cannot think in complex ways about teaching, learning, and the purpose of schools, then the school cannot. Only when the leader can grow, learn, and develop in complex ways will the school grow, learn, and develop—and open the door to deep change.

WHAT WAS IT ALL ABOUT?

This is a complicated book. It is full of complicated theory, practitioners' stories, advice from school leaders, and practical tools. It makes a complicated argument, and at the end even gives some contradictory advice. It describes a powerful Common Theory and offers an UnCommon Theory in response—the deep dive. The book covers a lot of ground. So, at the end, what was it all about?

This book argues that the work of reinventing schools into more equitable places has been seriously underestimated. Despite frequent "calls to action," "bold moves," and "groundbreaking initiatives," the predictive value of race, class, sexual identity, and language remains largely unchanged (Farkas, 2017). The Common Theory has been persistently applied to the work of reinventing schools, and when that theory has been found inadequate, a newer version of the Common Theory—Common Theory plus a sense of urgency—was offered. Turning up the heat has not helped.

The reason we educators have not reinvented schools is not because we do not want to, but because we cannot—or we do not think we can. We often don't know how to stay in hard conversations. We don't always value dissenting voices. We don't typically sit with unanswered questions, or surface and explore fundamental assumptions. We can't because we often have not done the adult development work that Jed Lippard did at Prospect Hill Academy, or that Cathy O'Connell and Michael Maloney did at North Reading Middle School. We can't because, unlike Liz Ozuna or Matt Underwood or Deirdre Williams or Andres Lopez, we too easily ignore uncomfortable facts about inequitable practices or low expectations for students. We can't because, unlike Deb Holman at Brookline High School or Andy Plemmons at Barrow Elementary, we are afraid of a future, which has not yet arrived, but surely must.

The deep dive offers us a way to think about and build that future, to find a new way of being in schools, and to reinvent schools so that every child is successful.

References

Aguilar, E. (2013). *The art of coaching: Effective strategies for school transformation*. San Francisco, CA: John Wiley & Sons.

Asia Society. (2018). Center for Global Education: International Studies Schools Network. Retrieved from asiasociety.org/international-studies-schools-network

Bachman, J. G., Staff, J., O'Malley, P. M., & Freedman-Doan, P. (2013). Adolescent work intensity, school performance, and substance use: Links vary by race/ethnicity and socioeconomic status. *Developmental Psychology, 49*(11), 2125–2134.

Barth, R. S. (2006). Improving relationships within the schoolhouse. *Educational Leadership, 63*(6), 8–13.

Benitez, M., Davidson, J., & Flaxman, L. (2009). *Small schools, big ideas: The essential guide to successful school transformation*. San Francisco, CA: Jossey-Bass.

Blase, R., Blase, J., & Philips, D. Y. (2010). *Handbook of school improvement: How high-performing principals create high-performing schools*. Thousand Oaks, CA: Corwin Press.

Braidotti, R. (2013). *The posthuman*. Cambridge, United Kingdom: Polity Press.

Bransford, J. D., Brown, A. L., & Cocking, R. R. (2000). *How people learn: Brain, mind, experience, and school*. Washington, DC: National Academy Press.

Breidenstein, A., Fahey, K., Glickman, C., & Hensley, F. (2012). *Leading for powerful learning: A guide for instructional leaders*. New York, NY: Teachers College Press.

Bryk, A. S. (2015). Accelerating how we learn to improve. *Educational Researcher, 44*(9), 467–477.

Bryk, A. S., Gomez, L. M., Grunow, A., & LeMahieu, P. G. (2015). *Learning to improve: How America's schools can get better at getting better*. Cambridge, MA: Harvard Education Press.

Bryk, A. S., Sebring, P. B., Allensworth, E., Luppescu, S., & Easton, J. Q. (2010). *Organizing schools for improvement: Lessons from Chicago*. Chicago, IL: University of Chicago Press.

Bush, G. W. (2004, September 2). *Text: President Bush's acceptance speech to the Republican National Convention*. Retrieved from www.washingtonpost.com/wp-dyn/articles/A57466-2004Sep2.html

Carter, K. (2017). Five dispositions for personalization. *Educational Leadership, 74*(6), 75–78.

Chung Wei, R., Darling-Hammond, L., & Adamson, F. (2010). *Professional development in the United States: Trends and challenges*. Dallas, TX: National Staff Development Council.

Clinton, W. J. (2000, January 27). *Address before a joint session of the Congress on the state of the union.* Retrieved from www.presidency.ucsb.edu/documents/address-before-joint-session-the-congress-the-state-of-the-union-7

Cooperrider, D., & Whitney, D. (2005). *Appreciative inquiry: A positive revolution in change.* San Francisco, CA: Berrett-Koehler.

Cousins, E. (2000). *Roots: From outward bound to expeditionary learning.* Dubuque, IA: Kendall/Hunt.

Cuban, L. (2003). *Why is it so hard to get good schools?* New York, NY: Teachers College Press.

Cuban, L., & Usdan, M. (2002). *Powerful reforms with shallow roots: Improving America's urban schools.* New York, NY: Teachers College Press.

Darling-Hammond, L. (2010). *The flat world and education: How America's commitment to equity will determine our future.* New York, NY: Teachers College Press.

DiCamillo, K. (2013). *Flora and Ulysses: The illuminated adventures.* Somerville, MA: Candlewick Press.

Donohoo, J., Hattie, J., & Eells, R. (2018). The power of collective efficacy. *Educational Leadership, 75*(6), 40–44.

Drago-Severson, E. (2009) *Leading adult learning: Supporting adult development in our schools.* Thousand Oaks, CA: Corwin Press.

Dunne, F., Evans, P., & Thompson-Grove, G. (2018). Consultancy. In *School Reform Initiative* [Website]. Retrieved from www.schoolreforminitiative.org/download/consultancy/

Elmore, R. F. (2004). *School reform from the inside out: Policy, practice, and performance.* Cambridge, MA: Harvard Education Press.

Eubanks, E., Parish, R., & Smith, D. (1997). Changing the discourse in schools. In P. Hall (Ed.), *Race, ethnicity, and multiculturalism: Policy and practice* (pp. 151–168). New York, NY: Garland.

Fahey, K. (2012). Where principals dare to dream: Critical friends group narrows the gap between vision and reality. *Journal of Staff Development, 33*(3), 28–30.

Farkas, G. (2017). *Human capital or cultural capital?: Ethnicity and poverty groups in an urban school district.* New York, NY: Routledge.

Fraser, E. (2017). School walk protocol. In *School Reform Initiative* [Website]. Retrieved from www.schoolreforminitiative.org/download/school-walk-protocol/

Gergen, K. J. (2014). From mirroring to world-making: Research as future forming. *Journal for the Theory of Social Behavior, 45*(3), 287–308.

Goodlad, J. (2004). *A place called school* (2nd ed.). New York, NY: McGraw-Hill.

Guskey, T. R., & Yoon, K. S. (2009). What works in professional development? *Phi Delta Kappan, 90*(7), 495–500.

Hargreaves, A., & Shirley, D. (2009). The persistence of presentism. *Teachers College Record, 111*(11), 2505–2534.

Heifetz, R. A. (1994). *Leadership without easy answers.* Cambridge, MA: Harvard University Press.

Heifetz, R. A., Grashow, A., & Linsky, M. (2009). *The practice of adaptive leadership: Tools and tactics for changing your organization and the world.* Boston, MA: Harvard Business School.

Heifetz, R. A. & Linsky, M. (2004). When leadership spells danger. *Educational Leadership, 61*(7), 33–37.

Ippolito, J. (2013). Professional learning as the key to linking content and literacy instruction. In J. Ippolito, J. F. Lawrence, & C. Zaller (Eds), *Adolescent literacy in the era of the Common Core: From research into practice* (pp. 215–234). Cambridge, MA: Harvard Education Press.

Kegan, R. (1998). *In over our heads: The mental demands of modern life.* Cambridge, MA: Harvard University Press.

Kegan, R., Lahey, L. L., Miller, M. L., Fleming, A., & Helsing, D. (2016). *An everyone culture: Becoming a deliberately developmental organization.* Boston, MA: Harvard Business School.

Kramer, S. V., & Schuhl, S. (2017). *School improvement for all: A how-to guide for doing the right work.* Bloomington, IN: Solution Tree.

Kurtz-Costes, B., Swinton, A., & Skinner O. D. (2014). Racial and ethnic gaps in the school performance of Latino, African American, and White Students. In F. T. L. Leong, L. Comas-Díaz, G. C. Nagayama Hall, V. C. McLoyd, & J. E. Trimble (Eds). *APA handbook of multicultural psychology, Vol. 1: Theory and research* (pp. 231–246). Washington, DC: American Psychological Assocation.

Lewin, K. (1947). Group decision and social change. In G. E. Swanson, T. M. Newcomb, & E. L. Hartley (Eds.), *Readings in Social Psychology* (pp. 197–211). New York, NY: Holt.

Littky, D. (2004). *The big picture: Education is everyone's business.* Alexandria, VA: ASCD.

Lortie, D. C. (1975). *Schoolteacher: A sociological study.* Chicago, IL: University of Chicago Press.

McDonald, J. P. (2014). *American school reform: What works, what fails, and why.* Chicago, IL: University of Chicago Press.

McDonald, J. P., Isacoff, N. M., & Karin, D. (2018). *Data and teaching: Moving beyond magical thinking to effective practice.* New York, NY: Teachers College Press.

McDonald, J. P., & Allen, D. (2017). Tuning protocol. In *School Reform Initiative* [Website]. Retrieved from www.schoolreforminitiative.org/download/tuning-protocol/

McDonald, J. P., Mohr, N., Dichter, A., & McDonald, E. (2013). *The power of protocols: An educator's guide to better practice* (3rd ed.). New York, NY: Teachers College Press.

Mezirow, J. (2000). *Learning as transformation: Critical perspectives on a theory in progress.* San Francisco, CA: Jossey-Bass.

Obama, B. (2009, February 24). *Remarks of President Barack Obama—address to joint session of Congress.* Retrieved from obamawhitehouse.archives.gov/the-press-office/remarks-president-barack-obama-address-joint-session-congress

Positive Behavioral Interventions and Support (PBIS). (2018). Multi-tiered system of support (MTSS) & PBIS: What is multi-tiered system of support (MTSS)? Retrieved from www.pbis.org/school/mtss

Rose, D. H., & Meyer, A. (2006). *A practical reader in Universal Design for Learning.* Cambridge, MA: Harvard Education Press.

Safir, S. (2018). The emergent power of teacher leaders. *Educational Leadership, 75*(6), 69–73.

Sarason, S. (1996). *Revisiting the culture of the school and the problem of change.* New York, NY: Teachers College Press.

Scharmer, C. O. (2006, September/October). Theory U: Leading from the future as it emerges: The social technology of presencing. In *Fieldnotes* (The Shambhala Institute for Authentic Leadership), pp. 1–13. Retrieved from www2. waisman.wisc.edu/naturalsupports/pdfs/summer/Theory.pdf

Scharmer, C. O. (2009). *Theory U: Leading from the future as it emerges: The social technology of presencing.* San Francisco, CA: Berrett-Koehler.

Scharmer, C. O. (2018). *The essentials of Theory U: Core principles and applications.* Oakland, CA: Berrett-Koehler.

Schein, E. (2016). *Organizational culture and leadership* (5th ed.). San Francisco, CA: Jossey-Bass.

School Reform Initiative. (2018a). ATLAS: Learning from student work. In *School Reform Initiative* [Website]. Retrieved from www.schoolreforminitiative.org/ download/atlas-learning-from-student-work-protocol/

School Reform Initiative. (2018b). Collaborative Assessment Conference. In *School Reform Initiative* [Website]. Retrieved from www.schoolreforminitiative.org/ download/collaborative-assessment-conference/

School Reform Initiative. (2018c). Compass points: North, south, east, and west: An exercise in understanding preferences in group work. In *School Reform Initiative* [Website]. Retrieved from www.schoolreforminitiative. org/download/compass-points-north-south-east-and-west-an-exercise-in-understanding-preferences-in-group-work/

School Reform Initiative. (2018d). Text rendering experience. In *School Reform Initiative* [Website]. Retrieved from www.schoolreforminitiative.org/ download/the-text-rendering-experience/

Sizer, T. R. (2004). *Horace's compromise: The dilemma of the American high school* (4th ed.). New York, NY: Houghton Mifflin.

Sizer, T. R. & Sizer, N. F. (1999). *The students are watching: Schools and the moral contract.* Boston, MA: Beacon Press.

Thompson-Grove, G. (2018a). Connections. In *School Reform Initiative* [Website]. Retrieved from www.schoolreforminitiative.org/download/connections/

Thompson-Grove, G. (2018b). Pocket guide to probing questions. In *School Reform Initiative* [Website]. Retrieved from www.schoolreforminitiative.org/ download/pocket-guide-to-probing-questions/

Thompson-Grove, G. (2018c). Student work gallery. In *School Reform Initiative* [Website]. Retrieved from www.schoolreforminitiative.org/download/ student-work-gallery/

Tienken, C. H., & Orlich, D. C. (2013). *The school reform landscape: Fraud, myth, and lies.* Lanham, MD: Rowman & Littlefield.

Tschannen-Moran, M., & Clement, D. (2018). Fostering more vibrant schools. *Educational Leadership, 75*(6), 28–33.

The World Café (2018). Design principles. Retrieved from www.theworldcafe. com/key-concepts-resources/world-cafe-method/

Index

About the Authors and the Educators Profiled

Angela Breidenstein is a professor of Education at Trinity University in San Antonio, Texas. She coordinates the secondary Master of Arts in Teaching teacher preparation program and works with four professional development schools to support the learning of the schools, their students, the teachers, and interns in teaching. She contributed to the founding of the School Reform Initiative and served on its board. She began her career teaching middle and high school social studies and German.

Kevin Fahey is professor emeritus at Salem State University in Salem, Massachusetts, where he coordinated programs in Educational Leadership. He continues to work with school leaders to use the tools of critical friendship, facilitative leadership, and equitable practice to lead student, adult, and organizational learning. He also spent 25 years as a middle school teacher, high school department chair, district curriculum coordinator, and elementary school principal. Kevin was also board chair of the School Reform Initiative Board of Directors, 2013–2015.

Frances Hensley was a founding member and director of the School Reform Initiative, a national organization that supports and promotes the learning of educators in transformational learning communities. She leads professional development in support of adult collaboration in schools and districts across the country and in international settings. For more than 20 years, she was a faculty member in the College of Education at Georgia State University, where she led K–12 school–university partnerships. She began her career as a special education teacher in rural north Georgia.

Jacy Ippolito is an associate professor and department chair of Secondary and Higher Education at Salem State University in Salem, Massachusetts, where he currently coordinates programs in Educational Leadership. Jacy's overlapping research interests include the roles that teachers, teacher leaders, principals, and literacy coaches play in helping institute and maintain instructional change at middle and high school levels. Before entering higher education, Jacy worked as a middle school reading specialist, drama teacher, and literacy coach in the Cambridge Public Schools, Cambridge, Massachusetts.

The Educators Profiled

Deborah Holman is the director of Elementary Special Education for the North Andover, Massachusetts Public Schools. She was the headmaster of Brookline High School in Brookline, Massachusetts, 2012–2016. She began her career in education in 1996 in Newton, Massachusetts.

Jed Lippard is the dean of Children's Programs at Bank Street College in New York, New York. Previously, he was the head of school of the Prospect Hill Academy Charter School in Somerville and Cambridge, Massachusetts, 2007–2016, and upper school principal, 2002–2007. He began his teaching career in 1995 at the Parker School in Devens, Massachusetts.

Andres Lopez teaches English and Mexican American literature courses at Stevens High School in San Antonio, Texas. He is the English Department coordinator and instructional coach, and he serves in other leadership roles in his school and community. He began his teaching career in 2001 in Austin, Texas, teaching middle school.

Michael Maloney is the assistant principal at North Reading Middle School in North Reading, Massachusetts. He began his career teaching English at North Reading Middle School, 2008–2010. Previously he taught at Austin Preparatory School in Reading, Massachusetts.

Cathy O'Connell is the principal of North Reading Middle School in North Reading, Massachusetts since 2011. Before that she was assistant principal of the Parker Middle School in Reading, Massachusetts, and also taught Grade 6 social studies.

Liz Ozuna is the executive director of Advanced Academics and Post-Secondary Access for the San Antonio Independent School District in San Antonio, Texas. She was the founding principal of the Mathis High School for International Studies in Mathis, Texas, 2007–2009, and provided ongoing support through 2012. She started teaching in 1996 in San Antonio at the International School of the Americas and also served as dean of English and Social Studies.

Andy Plemmons is the School Library Media Specialist at David C. Barrow Elementary School in Athens, Georgia. He has served in that role since 2008. He started his career in education as a classroom teacher in 2001.

Matt Underwood is the executive director of the Atlanta Neighborhood Charter School in Atlanta, Georgia. He served as that school's principal from 2007–2013 and also assumed the role of executive director in 2011. Matt continued to serve as executive director from 2011–2018. He began teaching in 1999 in Chicago.

Deirdre Williams is the leadership development officer for the Harris County Department of Education in Houston, Texas. She was the principal of Attucks Middle School in the Houston Independent School District, 2011–2015. She started teaching in 2004 in Houston.